A DREAM OF JEWELLED FISHES

A DREAM

OF

JEWELLED FISHES

REFLECTIONS ON ANGLING

JOHN ASTON

Aurum

First published in Great Britain 2007 by Aurum Press Ltd
7 Greenland Street, London NW1 0ND
www.aurumpress.co.uk

A catalogue record for the book is available
from the British Library.

ISBN-10: 1 84513 280 7
ISBN-13: 978 1 84513 280 4

1 3 5 7 9 10 8 6 4 2
2007 2009 2011 2010 2008

Text design by Peter Ward
Typeset in Adobe Caslon by Saxon Graphics, Derby
Printed and bound by MPG Books, Bodmin

This book is dedicated to the memory
of Len Grayson, fisherman:
the spark who lit the flame

CONTENTS

FOREWORD

One of the pleasantest things in the world is going a journey; but I like to go by myself

WILLIAM HAZLITT, 'On Going a Journey'

IT SEEMED A GOOD time to write this book; there was a collision of circumstances that needed to be exploited. I wrote the first chapter shortly after the clocks went back and we slid into winter; it is the right season in which to reflect – sometimes the only available light seems to shine from memory rather than actuality. And 2005 was the right year to start the book, which I had wanted to write since I had first had an article published in the early 1980s. Although I displayed all the arrogance of my generation – we thought that being middle aged was for older people and not for our gilded peers – turning fifty in 2002 did constitute a reality check on my planned immortality. And 2005 was a tough year to live through, for a host of reasons that have little place in a fishing book.

When I wrote the first chapter my intention was clear enough: this would be a fishing autobiography, starting in the West Riding, diverting through Lincolnshire, Scotland and returning to my North Yorkshire trout streams. I expected to consult fishing diaries, knew that I would spend hours poring over faded photographs in old albums and telephoning old acquaintances to check half forgotten memories. I guess this is what most proper authors would have done, believing that accuracy is important, that no fact should be given an emphasis that it does not deserve in absolute terms. I can write accurately when somebody pays me to, but I quickly realised that I wanted to treat the whole book as a series of memories interspersed with reflections on what seems important. Metaphor alert – and you're going to have to get used to it – think of this book as a trout stream rolling down from the high moors and then meandering through the plains. And, as you read, visualise the stream: see how it thunders over waterfalls, creeps through the deeps and eddies back on itself for reasons that are sometimes clear but often unfathomable. It can be difficult to navigate along it, but the journey itself can be fun. Forget the destination, let the current do its worst, but beware of unseen obstructions.

I only had one defining principle in writing this book – to describe how it felt. Sounds simple, but isn't; some feelings were pure recollections of the moment, but others are more reflective of what hindsight enables me to feel now. You will realise that the stream's flow carries not just water, but other stuff discarded further upstream, sometimes by me, sometimes by others.

Thanks to everybody who made this book possible; to the friends I have mentioned in the text, especially Neil Perry and the late Jon Stevens; to Len Grayson, to whom this book is dedicated and without whom . . . , etc. Thanks to Andrea Spence for typing the book and enduring my constant revisions and amendments, and thanks to Joanne, my wife, for understanding and accepting that fishing is about so much more than days on the river.

John Aston
Over Silton
June 2007

CHAPTER ONE

NO GURU, NO METHOD,
NO TEACHER

As no man is born an artist,
so no man is born an angler

Izaak Walton, *The Compleat Angler*

I HAVE NEVER BEEN aware of not being a fisherman. It is not a sport, nor a hobby, nor a pastime – it just is. There was no conscious awakening of interest as a child, no encouragement by well-meaning relative or family friend. But there was a fascination, an obsession, with water from the day I first could crawl towards it. As a two-year-old I would stare into the water butts in the garden and watch, captivated, as the bloodworm larvae thrashed in the green-tinged water. Twenty years would pass before I knew them as chironimids – or buzzers, as I called them before I became middle aged and inclined to pretension.

Home was a sprawling mining village in the West Riding of Yorkshire which was called Allerton Bywater; and it was indeed surrounded by water, but most of it was utterly lifeless. The streams were poisoned by opencast mines, and the River Aire, ten minutes' walk from home, ran thick with pollution and was capable of supporting only rats. The river contained immense quantities of suspended detergent from the wool mills upstream; on windy days great white lumps of foam would be blown through nearby Castleford's streets, and they would chase the pedestrians like malevolent clouds.

I was five when I was given my first rod; a birthday present from – whisper it – the family gardener, Ernest. And, yes, I did come from a family which had such things as retainers, cleaners and 'ladies who did'. Ernest was a retired miner, toothless and kind; wore tired shiny suits and collarless shirts. Like all miners, he had hands prickled dark blue from subcutaneous coal dust, and in repose he would sit low, resting on his heels to enjoy his Player's Navy Cut. I loved their smell, and I loved to see the untipped cigarettes lined up like crisp white soldiers in the packet. Ernest was born in 1890 and was a good friend to the village doctor's young son. Dad was a stranger to fishing, if not to country sports. He had shot geese with Peter Scott on the freezing flatlands of the Wash, he had stalked deer in India during the Second World War, and he hunted with the Badsworth for over forty years. I suspect – no, I know – that I was a disappointment to him. I had no interest in medicine, loathed horses and loved my own company more than others' – especially my father's. Things were always black or white from his perspective, but from mine they could be any shade – or many shades – in between, even from the earliest of ages. I would rather read a book than muck out a stable, and rather do just about anything than get on another dim-witted horse. I thought it ludicrous that, sixty years after the end of the War, he still signed his cheques 'C.E. Aston, Major, RAMC Retd'. So we weren't close, Dad and I, and that forced, or perhaps chosen, independence was essential in forging my own identity. Fishing was a very big part of this; it was something which I could do – did do – and he could not. Baggage? Hell, yes.

Ah . . . the rod. It was greenheart and the colour of an October chestnut, whipped in green and with an agate top ring. Three pieces, 10 feet, and much too heavy for a five-year-old. But we found a reel in our box room: a ghastly little metal centrepin which always seemed as though it was spinning in grit and sand – a Hardy it was not. And we visited the tackle shop in Castleford and we bought hideously unsuitable floats, line and hooks. I found brandling worms in the older horse muck in the garden, and I was ready to fish.

There was only one place to do this, a shallow pond next to the river, called The Pasture. We were in the West Riding, however, and inevitably it was pronounced t'Pastor. Reed mace surrounded the pond, which periodically was invaded by the Aire's floodwater, but somehow the fish survived, and the pond held a good head of roach, some tench and pike, and silver hordes of sticklebacks. Years would pass before I saw anything of the roach, or any fish at all other than the unsatisfactory and unfulfilling stickleback. I had no mentor or guide and I had yet to meet friends who shared my passion, and so for long years I lived in a sort of fishy desert, totally ignorant, always hopeful, but so very hungry for a proper fish. The fuel was there, but not a spark appeared until my father told me to visit Len, a patient who lived on the nearby Council estate.

And Len Grayson, to whom this book is dedicated, truly changed my life. He was another retired miner, and one of the smartest fishermen I have ever met. He never patronised his young protégé, never bored him either, as he would switch from instruction to reminiscence so seamlessly. He told me of the great bream of the Ouse, the barbel in the Wharfe, the grayling in the Costa, and, more relevantly, he told me about the fish he caught in t'Pastor. Roach, and big ones too. Len taught me about the need for fine tackle, self-cocking floats and chrysalids for bait – whatever they were. Over endless tea, punctuated by a steady march of Woodbine tippeds, Len described unknown dimensions to the pond that had become such a familiar, although unproductive haunt for me.

Unlike some of Dad's patients, Len was never deferential and he wasn't apprehensive about going to see him and telling him, firmly but politely, that he should buy me some decent tackle. Len gave him a shopping list, and Dad decided he would buy the gear but not allow me to use it until I was fourteen – four years away. I will always admire Len for standing up to Dad, telling him not to be stupid, asking him why he had bought me a pony which I loathed (look, the middle classes can suffer too), and suggesting that I use the gear now and fish at least twice a week. Len was truly a major influence and a man to whom I will always be grateful.

The new tackle, now it was available for use, was a joy; there was a 12-foot glass match rod, an Intrepid Monarch fixed-spool reel, a proper wicker basket and an aluminium maggot tin. All this was fairly state-of-the-art stuff for 1962, and the rod was the *pièce de résistance*. It was sensational, black with red whippings, and it felt as light as air after the dense greenheart. The next season, it caught fish on t'Pastor too.

Len had taught me how to bait up a swim with maggot and fine breadcrumb groundbait, told me to fish at dawn the following day with chrysalids, hooked invisibly on a Size 18 spade-end to nylon. I still have some of Len's self-cocking floats – I treasure them and will admit to just having checked their presence in my cabinet. Their form is dictated by function – slim, painted a pale matt green with a red tip; no bottom eye, just a neatly whipped nylon loop. I fished one of Len's floats on a warm misty morning in midsummer. In the distance I could hear the usual background hum from the pit and the throb and grumble of barges grinding their way up to Leeds against the current of the river. Closer by, I could hear the indignant scolding discourse of the coots and the contented mutterings of a pair of mallard. The float was shotted well down and barely visible above the silver rippled surface. After a short time it moved; in fact it positively darted. It dipped and then was dragged under, and it seemed almost supernatural, something that a boy should not really have witnessed, felt like being released from years of fantasy. And reality was so good when it was like this; I struck, and for the first time in my life I felt that electric jolting solidity of a fish. Cack-handedly I played the fish to my virgin landing net, triangular, alloy pole and orange netted, of course. I picked the fish up – a gorgeous silver blue roach, cold to the touch and with its docile mouth barely pricked by the tiny hook. Ten ounces, perhaps less. But very little can ever compare: it was the border I crossed to reach a lifetime of addiction, an imperative to repeat the sensation as often as I could.

Len died twenty years ago, and the pond is now a shrunken, sanitised version of its former self. There is no pit – Mrs Thatcher took care of that – and there are hardly any barges left on the river. But there is a clean Aire – and there's cleaner air too.

So this was the spark which lit the flame more than forty years ago. The almost mystical rivers that Len told me about became familiar haunts, and I have replicated my first catch thousands of times over. From the cold clean wilderness of north-west Sutherland to the ranunculus delight of the Kennet and the Avon, from the bleakness of a Fen drain in December to the green delight that is the River Rye in springtime, this book is about what I remember and what I cannot forget. (Those, incidentally, are not the same thing by a very long way.) This book is about growing up, both as an angler and as a man, but most of all it is about how it feels to be pierced by the emotion which this sport can offer you.

CHAPTER TWO

ORIENTEERING

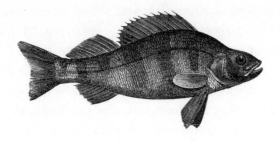

*Shine by the side of every path we tread
with such a lustre he who runs may read*

WILLIAM COWPER, 'Tirocinium'

T HERE IS A STRANGE imperative, as a fisherman, to move away from waters, even very good ones, which feel too close to home. Maybe the wanderlust is something about the importance of the journey, or about how travel time can be exploited to rehearse or to reflect upon the day, or perhaps it is a baser need simply to distance oneself from the familiar and immerse oneself in the remote and the strange. I have never wanted a river at the bottom of my garden; I fear it would quickly become as familiar, and as interesting, as my lawn – unless, of course, the river had changing levels and flows, changing populations of fish and a depth and breadth sufficient to intimidate me. The Tay would be fine, but a chalk stream would be little more than a water feature with all the ghastly connotations of suburbia which that involves.

So the wanderlust thing manifested itself worryingly early in my relationship with t'Pastor. I must have fished it many times,

6

but only the memory of the first success remains. And there were other lakes to discover around Allerton Bywater, heard about from friends, or acquaintances of friends' brothers. Some sounded like, and proved to be, myths, but one of the fantasy lakes turned out to be very real. It was called, with a startling lack of originality, the Green Lagoon, and getting there involved a forty-five-minute walk over a working railway.

Trucks full of coal and slag were pulled so slowly that their presence could be heard – and felt in the clicking lines – whole minutes before the train arrived. We stood back a yard or two and usually got a wave from the boiler-suited driver. Nowadays trains run quickly and evenly, but not then – so subsided was the ground from a century of coal working that the train would buck and heave like a trawler in an Atlantic swell. Towards the end of the line, literally, the sleepers were laid on raw grey slag. There were thousands – millions – of tons of the stuff, and it was spread for miles over what once had been attractive Yorkshire countryside. But in the middle of this wilderness of spoil lay a lake of extraordinary beauty. It was green, but you guessed that already; it was clear, deep and surrounded by a littoral band of rich, dark green weed. The lake covered perhaps 15 or 20 acres but the shoreline ran for long miles, so indented was it with bays and inlets, islands and promontories. It felt like the setting of an Enid Blyton story, so steeped was it in the potential for adventure.

Melvyn – my fishing friend – and I had heard that there were perch in the lake and arrived prepared with cloth bags full of lobworms in moss strung around our necks. We decided to fish a wooded bay; we lit our illicit Embassy tipped and we cast 5 yards out, just beyond the weedbeds. We had plumbed the depth and found 7 feet or more of water and our two quill floats sat riding out the ripples in the open water. After ten minutes my float dipped twice and then jerkily disappeared beneath the surface. I was not prepared for the violent charging of the 1lb-plus perch I had hooked. Roach can bend the rod, but this fish fought – and I had to learn quickly how to control a fish at close quarters, on a tight line. Despite, or because of the walk, the Green Lagoon became a regular haunt. We explored the banks and bays, we experimented with methods we had read about in Len's discarded *Angling Times* and we caught a lot of perch. Up to twenty a session, averaging ½lb to ¾lb; occasionally we caught fish of well over 1lb, and the biggest was almost 1¾lbs. We found that the bigger fish preferred free-lined lobworms, twitched, sink-and-draw style. Or we live-baited – with perch live-bait in fact.

Only rarely did we see another angler there. It became our own secret lake, but, despite the quality of sport, the Green Lagoon could prickle the spine. It was the only local water I never fished alone. It was surrounded by high walls of slag at its southern end and it was eerily silent, although, occasionally, great rolling slabs of slag would fall down the steep bank and splash malevolently into the lake. We had heard stories of two boys who had drowned in the lake, and we believed them only too easily. And the lake itself died shortly afterwards, the perch disease having arrived, and not a fish was to survive its blight. And curiously, perhaps even uniquely, the Green Lagoon held only the one species.

Rivers became my first love as soon as I fished one. Len and a couple of his fishing mates from the pit took me to Hunter's Lodge on the Yorkshire Ouse. Crushed into the back of a grey Morris Minor van, surrounded by creels and holdalls, it felt like, and was, a very long journey in every sense. I was with grown-ups who treated me as one of their own, and I was going to fish moving water for the first time. And the river was truly a revelation; it was a dull but warm day, and the river slid silently by. It had an organic, animate smell, utterly in contrast to the noxious chemical vapours of the Aire. Water voles paddled benignly across the 30 yards between its banks, and small fish stippled the surface constantly. Len knew how to teach – he had a hands-off style, and he put me in the right swim, told me the method and left me to learn and to enjoy. I had a day of days. I long trotted, using my punchily named Strikeright Aduraflo centrepin reel. First came the willow blades (as Len termed the ubiquitous bleak) and then the dace and the roach. Later still came that familiar jagging brawl of good-sized perch. I caught perhaps fifty or sixty fish that day, and I have loved trotting slow, deep water ever since.

Days like this gave me confidence I could bank. For years, fishing had been more of a faith thing for me, as actually catching fish – feeling them pull, holding them, feeling the weight of a good fish – all these things had never been experienced. And I couldn't even imagine what it was like. Yes, it was the cliché of the virgin reading pornography and finding it ultimately unsatisfactory because the subject matter was fantasy rather than an achievable reality.

I knew I would enjoy catching fish, of course, but the feeling of satisfaction and security that came from realising that the secret was simply the fact that there was no secret, made me comfortable, confident and suffused me with optimism about my next trip. And there were many, especially to the Ouse, when Dad could be persuaded to drive me there. And to credit him, he did often literally go out of his way to take me to the river and to collect me between surgeries. Maybe he had given up on the struggle to make me a replica of himself, a person upon whom he could project his own ambitions and recreate his own character. As I write, he died nine months ago, and whatever distance separated us for so many decades is probably a little less now.

Naburn Locks became my favourite venue. Here, some miles below York, the river is tidal, deep and wide. There is a weir too, which suffuses the air with that unique invigoration of ozone. There is something coarse, organic – almost sexual – about a weir pool, as though the movement of water creates another element,

intangible other than through a feeling of euphoria and near gid-
diness. On later trips we fished the weir pool at night, illegally
and dangerously, but my first Naburn trips were to the sand beds
below the Locks. The river's current changed with the tide, as did
the whole direction of flow.

We didn't have a Severn Bore equivalent, nor the lesser known
Trent wave, the Aegir, but the Ouse could still rise with startling
speed. Quick enough to maroon anglers, leaving them stranded
on muddy promontories and watching their wicker baskets float
towards Selby. The river fished best at the end of the high tide, as
the water lolled indecisively between ebb and flow. And the Ouse
was full of fish. Legering was an art yet to be acquired, but even
with our standard set-up of double maggot, Size 16 or 18, and a
stick or quill float, we caught a catholic selection of fish. First
would come the flashing willow blades, quick-biting and tiny,
and then, with regular loose feeding of maggots each cast, would
come the ultra-fast bites from dace, which had the enthusiasm of
the bleak but the fight of something better. Later still would
come the roach, which varied between a few ounces and perhaps
¾lb but they were, and still are, a sight truly to lift the heart.
There is something so quintessentially English about them – they
don't do anything dramatic, don't grow big or fight especially
hard, but they do have a feminine dignity which is utterly
irresistible.

When we tired, we would put our rods in a rod rest. Actually,
we didn't call them that, as in sixties' West Riding they were
called idlebacks. We would sit on our baskets, watching the float
lie almost parallel to the surface at the end of our swims. This
technique was called stret pegging in the few fishing books I had
acquired, but I never liked the term: it sounded military, ordered
and disciplined. We preferred the local term of 'odding back'.
Etymology aside, it worked superbly: the float would stab under
– hard, often with sufficient force to pull the rod tip around.

Bigger fish were often responsible, sometimes a 1lb chub, some-times a bream or a perch a little larger. But sometimes there were gudgeon, which have something of the appeal of the roach in their biddability, or, uninvited, the ghastly tommy ruffe. Ruffe had no appeal other than their bare status as fish and, as I write, it is probably twenty-five years since I have even seen a ruffe. Have they gone the way of the burbot, the vole and the unicorn?

Legering had drifted into my consciousness, and Peter Stone was probably to blame. Melvyn and I had read about the tech-nique in the *Angling Times*; we had seen grainy black-and-white photographs of enormous bags of bream from Witham, Welland and Thames, and we had read about the revolutionary swingtip method. One Christmas produced a 9-foot yellow glass Ernie Stamford swingtip rod, and on 1 June it made its debut on a swollen River Ouse, inevitably at Naburn. Why a six-month wait? And why the first of June, not the glory-steeped sixteenth? The answer to the first question is that I simply lacked the confi-dence to fish without a float in the hard, cold months of January and February (although decades of hindsight now make me realise it would have saved many a blank day). And the answer to the second question is the fact that the Yorkshire season then ended on 28 February and started on 1 June. And no, I do not remem-ber what we did in leap years. When you're sixteen, the frequency of leap years is low – they occur at intervals of 25 per cent of your lifespan. They don't now; they have assumed the depressing reg-ularity of general elections, the World Cup and other follies.

The Ouse was high, brown and flowing hard downstream. But the air was warm, and there was that feeling of absolute joy at the anticipation, and now realisation, of a nine-month season in which to indulge, starting here and now. I fished a slow, wide eddy, curiously similar to the illustrations of stylised eddies which graced the pages of Mr Crabtree. It didn't quite have the arrows pointing out where the fish lived but, in honesty, it didn't really need to, so obvious were the hotspots. Weed and debris on the line were a constant irritant that day, producing those hard draws on the rod tip which you so want to believe are real bites, but which you know lack the stabbing immediacy of the real thing. Usually . . . because yet another half-hearted strike produced the unexpected consequence of line being ripped from the clutch and a bucking rod tip. After a series of short, hard runs a weed-festooned coffin lead appeared, and below it was a barbel. The first we had ever seen, but immediately recognisable. We prized that fish and we loved its looks. There is something uniquely engaging about barbel, they have something of the appeal of a Labrador puppy; they are rounded, muscly and perfectly proportioned.

We knew from an *Angling Times* article that barbel loved weir pools, and later trips to the same venue included illicit trespass over the locks themselves. Under cover of darkness we would creep over the lock gates to fish in the weir pool itself. Depending upon the state of the tide, we sat up to 6 feet above the water on a hard concrete bank, surrounded by spray from the weir, ears deafened by the constant roar of tons of falling water.

Our method was simple, lobworms on Size 6 hooks on 6lb line, often fished right under the rod tip into the swirling, cross-currented pool. The river-bed was studded with stones and debris, and tackle losses were correspondingly high, but we caught fish too. More barbel, of course, up to 4lbs or so, giants for us in those days; but we also caught pike, flounders, eels and bream. Melvyn and I fished together closely, landing each other's fish and sharing the excitement of our new discovery.

It was now the early seventies, and my personal circumstances were changing. I had passed my driving test and my 'A' Levels too. University beckoned, and the friends I was to make there are with me still. And Melvyn? We lost touch for thirty years, and each of us often wondered what became of the other. We found out only a few months before this chapter was written. We are alive, we are well, and the talking was easy, unforced. And we have resolved to have a day on the river together soon. And who could ask for more than that?

CHAPTER THREE

CELTIC FRINGES

I will arise and go now, and go to Innisfree,
And a small cabin build there; of clay and wattles made

W.B. YEATS, 'The Lake Isle of Innisfree'

TODAY'S GP HOLIDAYS SOMEWHERE like the Seychelles, or perhaps a timeshare villa near an Alp. Sixties GPs were a little more parochial, especially if their fox-hunting habit consumed quite so much time and money. My family has many Irish connections, on both sides of the sectarian divide, and until the Troubles exploded in the late sixties, Donegal was a regular destination for family holidays. The journey was arduous, especially in an underpowered Humber Hawk towing a trailer full of provisions. Eire did have shops, of course, but not as cheap as those in the West Riding. And so our impact on the local economy was towards the light end of featherweight, confined principally to soda bread, milk and Harp lager.

We would take a day to get to Stranraer, and, in those days before roll-on roll-off, the black Humber was loaded on the ferry's deck by a net suspended beneath a derrick. This would add an element of uncertainty to the holiday, as the Humber pirouetted dangerously close to the masts and other maritime fixtures. The crossing was an even bigger adventure, though, because the Irish sea is famed for its temper, and Dad rarely missed the opportunity to remind us of the ferry which had sunk with all hands a decade before. The drive through Northern Ireland to Donegal was a delight, especially for a teenager unused to seeing policemen with sten guns. In those days the IRA were a historical footnote, and their main activities were confined to inept attempts to blow up bridges and postboxes. It was local colour – they hadn't started killing again then.

We stayed in the wild west on a sea lough called Lough Swilly, or even further west, at a hamlet called Marble Hill, which faced the Atlantic. In the sixties Ireland felt like a third-world country, tractors were often communally owned by villagers, widows wore black, and donkeys were ubiquitous. They broke the heart too, nowhere else have I ever seen such untended hooves – the poor brutes would stumble around the fields with 6 inches, even a foot, of untrimmed hoof furrowing the soil. Agriculture was little more than bare subsistence; the fields were tiny and the soil was unable to sustain a good harvest. At hay time there were no plastic-wrapped bales, no orange-string binding, but small mounds of hay left to dry in the moist Atlantic wind. And from the edges of the fields would always come that unmistakeable grating click of the corncrake. Donegal felt ancient, felt eerie, windswept and utterly bewitching. I was used to the muddy North Sea at Bridlington, and the sight and sound of huge Atlantic rollers crashing into the long deserted strand of Tramore was an elemental pleasure. Between the strands lay cliffs – Horn Head, Fanad Head – which were dotted with guillemot and razorbill, and out to sea lay the long dark profile of Tory Island, which sounds much better in its Gaelic manifestation of Oilean Toraigh; meaning Island of the Pirates. The story is that it was inhabited by the Fomorans, originally from Turkey, and their king was called Balor of Mighty Blows. Not a man to confront, as his one eye had to be kept covered except in anger, such was its force for destruction. His grandson, Lugh, representing goodness in Irish mythology, eventually killed the evil Balor, and in the sixth century Colm Cille converted the islanders and built a monastery there, surely a place to feel humbled in the endless battery of the Atlantic gales. Of course, it sounds quaint now, but it didn't then. There was a sinister, ancient rhythm to Donegal, and when my godmother told me of the seventh son of the seventh son with the second sight it didn't feel like a fairy story, it felt more like what passed for reality in that dreamtime place.

You felt much closer to America than the UK there; every home had a picture of John F. Kennedy as well as the inevitable print of Pope John, and the sitting room would be stocked with old *Saturday Evening Post*s sent by relatives living in Brooklyn or Boston. I would marvel at the advertisements for Studebakers and Stingrays, Chesterfields and Lucky Strikes. It was all so colourful, so confident – almost brash – and in such sharp contrast to the deferential conformity of our domestic *Telegraph* and *Express*. One night Dad and I were walking along a wild strand, where earlier we had found the washed-up remains of a killer whale; we saw a young girl, seven or eight, wading into the thunderous surf alone. We ran to her, we walked her back from the rollers, and through sobs she told us that her dad was in America, that she missed him and wanted to be with him across the water. We returned her to her home which was little more than a collection of hovels under the cliff.

The sea played a major part in our holidays, but never in a piscatorial sense. But two incidents still burn bright. The villagers of

Marble Hill had a curragh – little more than a boat-shaped skeleton but, instead of a wooden or fibreglass body, the curragh was made of tarred paper – typically newspaper upon which hot tar was poured from a smoking bucket. It worked, in a fashion, and I remember being amazed at how easily the featherweight craft would glide over the waves. No rod-and-line fishing, but a net rowed 50 or 60 yards out from the shoreline and then pulled back by two teams of men on the shore. We caught mullet – big ones too. We were given a huge grey mullet of 5lbs or more, and it tasted wonderful. Marble Hill also produced my only encounter with a live whale. I was walking down to the strand after lunch and could see an immense shape like a stranded boat, but clearly alive as it thrashed and turned in the shallows. It was a pilot whale, and it had come ashore to die. Perhaps 20 feet long, feeling like animated rubber but somehow unthreatening, almost responsive. I remembered helping to hold the whale in the water with the locals before we towed him out to sea again and again. Always in vain, though, as he would surf back into the shore until all life was gone.

I did fish with rod and line in Donegal, although not always with a reel. My first trip was with some tinker lads who promised that we would catch white trout from one of the peaty streams flowing from the heights of one of the local mountains, Muckish. I had the 10-foot greenheart with me, and the tinkers told me it was far too long, so instead I fished, reel-less, with the top two sections only. A few feet of nylon were knotted to the tip ring and, crawling low over the rock and heather, I was instructed how to lower the worm into the pool below. It was curious sport, uninvolving somehow, as I was told to keep well back from the bank and most of the time could not even see the water. I was told where to fish, when to strike and my only contribution was to lift the jiggling rod when instructed. The fish were sea trout, but tiny things of a few ounces.

Much better sport came when I was left to my own devices. I found Lough Kindrum, which had a good enough reputation to require a day ticket from the local hotel; whilst no Corrib nor Mask, Lough Kindrum was big enough to intimidate me, with a long and uneven rocky shoreline. Using the same tactics as for Green Lagoon perch, I freelined worms on Size 10 or 12s, using a couple of BB shot as casting weight. I cast to rising fish – why not? – and, although the hatch was clearly not being matched, I caught tough fighting brown trout to over 1½lbs. It was my first experience of wild fish and wild places, and it is a taste that has yet to desert me. And an abiding image of the Lough remains; fish had started to rise hard, probably to olives, and from the single-track road behind me I heard the familiar whistling clatter of a VW Beetle. The car stopped quickly, and out stepped a cassocked priest; he leant into the back of the car and produced a split-cane fly rod. Within minutes he had caught a brace of trout and continued on his pastoral rounds. A simple country living made flesh?

And then there was Wales. The Troubles had elbowed us out of Ireland, and the sharp edges of Donegal were replaced by the gentler curves of the Lleyn peninsula. We stayed for three weeks most summers in Aberdaron, a village bisected by a trout stream, and it was there that I learnt how to upstream worm, a technique I had read about in *A Boy Goes Trouting*. (A book, incidentally, which has not stood the test of time very well. It describes an upper-middle-class utopia: a perfectly ordered world where the ghillies, although patronised, were salt-of-the-earth yeomen but poachers were ruffians and scoundrels – or 'rough sorts' as the book termed them when describing how one should puncture their tradesman's van's petrol tank before calling the police. It did counsel against lighting the fuel, not on the grounds of safety or legality, but because the flames might attract the attention of the poachers.) But . . . the author knew his trout, if not virtually everything else, and I grew to love the intimacy of small-stream trout fishing.

Aberdaron's stream was rarely much more than 10 feet wide, usually less than a foot deep, but it was alive with hungry brown trout. They did not run to any significant size – a half-pounder was an event – but they were fast-biting, quick-witted fish which made me do some serious thinking about what I was doing and why. Up to then I had either done what I was told when fishing or followed what everyone else did, but here there *was* no one else – I never saw another angler on the water – and I had to work out the location of the fish myself and how to catch them. It was absorbing, revealing sport, and it took me miles up the valley away from the village. I suppose it must have been private water, but as it was so well hidden from sight, I didn't really care. The fish tasted good too, in those more innocent days of catch and kill.

When the rains came, the stream changed character. You can read about it in the next chapter – but suffice to say that the end was tearful.

Sea fishing featured too. Dad had pragmatically assumed that, as a fisherman, the more fish I could catch the happier I would be. He had made friends with a local fisherman called Robin John and stayed friends with him until his death. Robin John would take us out into the wild waters beyond the haven of Aberdaron Bay towards Bardsey Island, where, apparently, no less than 20,000 Welsh saints were buried. A surfeit of Dais . . . and I confess to a raised eyebrow at the prospect of 20,000 saints of any nationality.

Even launching the boat could be spectacular; Robin John would roll up his grey flannel trousers to his thighs, and we would push the clinker-built 15-footer straight out in the waves. On a rough day the boat would rear almost vertically as it encountered the first breakers, and we would paddle hard to get more depth under us before the Seagull outboard was started. The fishing itself was bountiful, as we were there in the high summer when the sea was full of mackerel. We would use handlines with feathers, pulled down deep by homemade leads. Each line would have up to fourteen feathers, and on a good night we would pull up fourteen fish every time, once we had located the shoals. It was little more than harvesting, but I loved that hard electric rapping on the fingers holding the handline as first one, then two, and then a whole string of mackerel would hit the feathers. Out into the sound between Bardsey Island and the headland called Braich y Pwll the sea would foam into oily, fast-flowing rivers of current where we would catch pollack and coalfish up to 4–5lbs. But the most spectacular sight was two basking sharks, both much longer than the boat, working the plankton shoals with their huge brown backs cleaving through the waves.

The night when we caught 600 mackerel, their weight pushing the boat down to its gunwales, finally made me realise that less really could be more. We sold the fish for a penny each, but I felt guilt and a mounting sense of disgust at the pointlessness of our plunder. More was never better; what mattered was not the number but the circumstances of the capture. And so I left the two men to their harvesting of the bay and I started to explore the rocky inlets along the peninsula. There were many tiny bays – Porth Isco, Porth Golmon and Fisherman's Cove – and all of them were flanked by steep cliffs jutting out into the Irish Sea over the deep clear water. At first I spun, with cheap, heavy spoons, fished sink-and-draw style over the kelp beds 30 feet down. The takes, when they came, were spectacular as pollack punched into the lures and crash-dived for the seabed. I lost plenty of fish but I caught them up to 4lbs; they were a beautiful golden brown, and they looked so tough, almost coarse, with their jutting lower jaws and their big eyes.

Later I learnt how to fish a sliding float, using mackerel strip or mussel for bait. The floats were the size of my live-baiting bungs, and I loved to watch them ride the rolling waves ten yards out from the base of the cliffs. I loved the waves themselves, their regular rhythmic crash into unyielding rock; and I loved to lick my lips to taste the salted spray. Dad had told me that the waves had a regular cycle resulting in the seventh wave always being the biggest, and, whilst I suspected a certain degree of folklore, the fact was that every few minutes a great rolling bruiser of a wave would curl over and surge hard up the rock towards me. Fishing in such vast waters, compared to the almost stifling intimacy of my trout stream, could intimidate, and feel like a game of chance played in the hope that coincidence would result in a fish being somewhere near the bait at the right time. But the game became easy to play when I concentrated on the area immediately next to the rocky outcrops and allowed the float to drift across the deep channels where the blue water would turn black. Wrasse became a favourite species, feeling almost like an alien seagoing perch, with their coarse scales and spined fins. Their mouths were unique, though, narrow-lipped and filled with teeth designed to grind down the toughest mollusc. They fought just like perch, all dash and jag and jolt.

Writing this, I realised just how many years have passed since I fished from the rocks, watched the choughs wheel over the cliff, watched the white gannets spear into the shoals of sprat and sand eel, and how long it is since I exchanged stares with the bowler-hatted seals, with their whiskered gaze of enquiry. I am not the first to say that I must go down to the sea again; but I must – and I shall.

CHAPTER FOUR

SNATCHING DEFEAT . . .

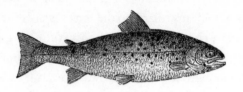

Who holds that if way to the Better there be,
it exacts a full look at the Worst

THOMAS HARDY, 'In Tenebris – II'

A CERTAIN PERCENTAGE OF hooked fish is lost; and a smaller percentage of hooked fish is large. Distil those numbers down, and the average angler will lose very few huge fish over the average career. All the same, whilst modesty would prevent me from characterising myself as anything much more than a very average fisherman, I have lost a number of big fish. Some of them were almost certainly big in an absolute sense – the Rutland trout was staggering – but others were just big in context. They hurt just as much, still produced that feeling of stunned disbelief, just as when you carelessly break a crystal wine glass. There is that illogical, but pressing feeling of refusing to accept what your senses are telling you, until slowly this is replaced by the angry desire for the clock to be reversed – just for a minute – so the tragedy would not have happened. But, if it were reversed, how would you know? Would I be a different fisherman, you a different reader and would the fish swim in a different stream? Perhaps some of our triumphs are actually due to neat, self-contained little reversals whose occurrence erases previous tragedies?

And this is what happens when time does not reverse.

I wrote about my Welsh trout stream in an earlier chapter. With the passing of each holiday at Aberdaron I became more proficient, to the degree where I could promise the family that there would be trout for tea. I would explore further upstream, and I found pools and runs which had possibly not been fished for years. I do regret now that I wasn't a fly fisherman back then, but another ten years would pass before that Damascene conversion. I knew the stream well, or so I thought, until one day it rained. Very heavily: a summer downpour. The hills were drenched with rain, and all of it coursed down to the swollen stream. I fished in the middle of the village that day, as to go upstream seemed pointless, given the brown spate that greeted me. The water was falling, quickly, but was still almost a foot higher than normal. Some years before I had fished the Upper Ure in Wensleydale with a school friend, and his uncle, with whom we stayed, virtually marched us to the river in similar conditions, as he assured us that these were the perfect conditions in which to catch good trout – on worm of course. So that shred of memory gave me a little confidence that day.

I was fishing a 9-foot split-cane combination rod – it doubled, disastrously, as a spinning and fly rod. It was the master of neither discipline. Preferring the greater length, I fished the rod in its fly-fishing manifestation, with the Intrepid fixed spool reel mounted right down at the butt of the rod. It was ungainly but it was useable. I fished 4lb Bayer line and a Size 10 hook, weighted down by a couple of AA shot. The hook was tied on with what should have been a blood knot but in reality was some ghastly home-brewed variation on a reef knot – good for string, or rope, but perhaps not quite as effective for thin monofilament. Still, it had never let me down in my epic struggles with ¼lb brownies.

I cast across and upstream, and within seconds the line held in my left fingers was tapped hard and then ripped against the reel. This had not happened before. Shocked, I struck into a heavy, fast-moving fish which immediately tail walked around the pool with a speed and violence which amazed me. It was silver and it was, of course, a sea trout. It would have smelled the fresh flowing water rushing out into the bay the previous night and would have swum hard and fast up to this, the first main pool above the tide. The trout was perhaps 1lb, and our acquaintance was brief, as its acrobatics enabled it to throw the hook in mid-leap.

The next cast produced a similar experience – bang, leap, slack. And the next a small, familiar and suddenly quite unwelcome brownie. But the next cast – something completely outside my experience happened. I had allowed the worm to drift close into my side of the pool. There was not a bite as such, just a sudden awareness that something heavy and unstoppable had taken the worm and was creaking the split cane into a semi-circle. I did not have a clue about playing fish properly; I had read about it but it was an experience then so far divorced from my personal reality that I couldn't translate it into a tactic. The clutch of my reel was screwed down far too tight and consequently the fish was given not an inch. I dragged the fish closer in towards the bank. Hadn't a clue how to land it as, netless, I had never really landed anything which couldn't be swung in. Unlike its predecessors this fish did not leap but it did thrash. Furiously. Spray erupted from the stream, soaking me, yet still I could not see the fish. And I never did. You will have guessed – my ropy apology of a hook knot had betrayed me. The Judas knot had unravelled, leaving a curled piece of nylon as its last witness.

I convinced myself that I had lost a salmon, although, of course, it was a good sea trout, I have no doubt. I discovered later that the owner of our holiday cottage had caught them up to 8lbs from the same stream. I never fished the stream in spate again – but I never tied a bad knot either. Suddenly those incomprehensible diagrams in my fishing books were not only important, they were necessary, and they demanded a translation.

In the mid-1960s, as a teenager, I stayed often with my aunt and uncle in Essex. Their son, Guy, my cousin, was only a little older than I was, and although he did not have the same drive, the imperative to fish as I did, he would come with me down to the local river, the Blackwater. It was a river outside my then experience; rivers in Yorkshire didn't look as though they belonged in a Constable painting. The river was clear, slow-moving and studded with swaying bands of weed. This river even had a mill pond, a feature often found in Mr Crabtree, but something I had never encountered until then.

We fished on a grey blustery day; the wind was at our backs, and the mill pond was as calm as such things are supposed to be, as it lay 5 feet below the ancient brick banks. Casting was difficult, for the pool was surrounded by trees, and an underarm flick was often all that was possible. But it was all that was needed, too, because the pool was deep close in to the bank. We fished lobworm, either whole or in short segments, under a red quill float, and we fished hard on the bottom, as our past visits had shown us that the small chub and gudgeon preferred a static bait to a moving one. Guy and I caught our usual quota of willing gudgeon, and the day was taking a predictable course: enjoyable, but not one that would be remembered in a month's time, and certainly not forty years later.

And then my float dipped twice and, so gently yet so firmly, was pulled diagonally under the pool's surface. The trees behind me – fatally, I came later to realise – prevented an assertive strike and I simply tightened into what I expected to be another blue-sheened gudgeon. It even felt like a gudgeon for a moment, until I realised that the distant wriggling that was being semaphored into the rod tip meant that my fish was actually swimming towards me. He was, too, and when he broke the surface and wallowed, head twisting and spined dorsal erect, Guy and I were awestruck.

A perch, of course, the easiest fish to recognise, but its scale was beyond our comprehension. Memorably, Dick Walker said that a big perch doesn't look just big, but bloody enormous. And this one was gigantic. The answer to the obvious question, even allowing for the inaccuracy of youth and the passage of time, I would say lay nearer to 4lbs than three. Guy had stretched down on the bank to lower the net to the water. Not necessary. The hook pulled out and the float shot into the trees behind me. We could not fish any more that day. The loss of that fish hurt like an open wound for days, weeks. And I have never seen a perch to equal it.

At the tip of the Hambleton peninsula at Rutland Water is a narrow creek. The sort of place that anglers who have a confidence problem with big waters naturally gravitate towards. Anglers like me, in fact. But that hot July day in 1978 had attracted a shoal of fish into the bay, well weeded up by that time of year. Fish were doing those lazy, oily head-and-tail rolls that are so characteristic of a buzzer hatch. Jon Stevens and I had become almost proficient at buzzer fishing by then, we had read Arthur Cove and Bob Church, and we had learnt the creed of the nymph fisherman – concentrate hard, fish slowly and strike if your instinct suggests you should. The fish continued to feed but our buzzer patterns failed to attract a take.

Jon and his wife, Cathy, disappeared to Oakham to find lunch. I fished on and I started to experiment. Not really in an intelligent way, but in the random, artless fashion which characterises a fisherman who has run out of ideas. If I had thought more carefully about what I was watching – observed the water rather than looking at it – I might have cracked the code, because there was no buzzer hatch at all, but there was a migration of floating snails. But as I was wilfully ignorant of this, I tied on a Size 12 Invicta, a fly I have always trusted to get me out of a jam. Reputedly it looks like a hatching sedge. Perhaps – I think it looks more like an olive, but it certainly doesn't look like a snail, even in a bad light.

So there was no real reason for the fact that my second cast retrieve was stopped solidly after a couple of yards had been figure-of-eighted into my left hand. At that time I was going through my weapons-grade phase of trout fishing and fished a 9ft 6in Conoflex No. 8 fibreglass rod, long belly floater and a leader of 7–8lbs point. Not an outfit which would normally be outgunned . . . but it was this time. It was a fight so one-sided as to be almost risible. I stayed put – I didn't have an alternative – and the trout simply decided to get as far away from me as possible. The first run took the line down to the backing. I didn't stop the run but the fish decided to rest, to catch its breath before disappearing towards the distant dam. Thirty yards of backing disappeared. The fish was now 60 yards away, but the rod tip was still being bullied into vicious stabs by this apparently unstoppable fish. The final run – another 20 yards disappeared. Not much backing left. But then slackness. Hopelessly I convinced myself that the trout had changed direction and was running back towards me. I reeled and reeled furiously. The line came back festooned in flags of weed and debris. And on the end was no trout, although the Invicta was still there.

She had done her best, but the strain had been too great for the thin wire and the hook had straightened. How big was that fish? A lot bigger than any trout I have ever hooked since, and a brown trout too, I suspect, given the determination of the fight and the absence of leaps.

There are many candidates for the most beautiful loch in Scotland. There is the obvious – such as the almost clichéd perfection of Loch Maree, or the wild edginess of Assynt or Hope, or perhaps the glaucous charm of Borralaidh. If you read Bruce Sandison's book on *Trout Lochs of Scotland*, you will find a score of other candidates. Or perhaps you have your own favourite, some hidden hill loch on Knoydart or a boulder-strewn lochan hanging up in the corries of Ben Klibreck or Ben Loyal. But to me there is one loch which is pre-eminent and that is Sionascaig.

If nothing else she (and this loch demands the feminine) has the name which is the most haunting, the most fey. You can read more about Skink a Kink, its prosaic alter ego, in Chapter Seventeen, but in this one I shall tell you about my tussle with a *Salmo ferox*. You have read BB's *A Fisherman's Bedside Book*? Of course, and you will have read the inspiring accounts of fishing for the most brutal and uncompromising of British game fish: the massive, mysterious and elusive cannibal trout, which prey on char in the cold deep lochs of the far north. Fish whose size can exceed any expectation of what a big trout should be: 20lbs, sometimes nearer 30lbs. Fishing for these near-mythical creatures demands huge dedication, specialist equipment and more time than most of us dare give to only the chance of a fish. My encounter was as memorable as it was unexpected. Ironically, it was almost light-hearted, and if I had landed the fish I should not really have deserved it.

We had fished Sionascaig hard and well that day, rowed up the length of loch, drifted into the deserted rocky bays, and we had caught perhaps a score of fish on Loch Ordies and Black Pennells. Sated, pressure off, we rowed back towards Boat Bay but noticed an abandoned boat on the shoreline. It was little longer than my fly rod and hopelessly unsuited for this wild water. We rowed to the shore and attached the tiny *Mary Celeste* to our sturdier craft. Neil (Perry) and Steve (Fox) stayed in the mother ship, and I precariously stepped into the bathtub boat. I took a rod, of course, Neil's 11-foot pike rod, armed with a planing lead and a Big S plug. I lowered the lure into the brown, peat-stained water and settled back for the tow home. There was plenty of good-natured ribaldry between our triumvirate – we were old and good friends who had fished together so often that we felt like a family, and the script was entirely predictable. That is, until the plot took a very odd turn when the rod tip banged over. Hard – in fact more than that: it felt downright malicious. It could only have been a fish, even though that was, in truth, the last thing I had expected. Laughing stopped as I tightened into something heavy and angry thirty feet beneath the boat. I pumped and gained the odd couple of yards but the fish ran deeper and regained them. And then, unexpectedly, the trout surfaced and leaped. Not a pretty fish, hook jawed, a darker shade of brown and somehow almost alien-looking. Not even a very big *ferox*, perhaps 4–5lbs. The head-shaking leap threw the barbless treble out of its jaws. And it didn't really feel so much a fish lost as an experience gained.

Barbel are not fish that are easy to lose, except on snags. They are almost – but not quite always – well hooked in their fleshy, almost humanoid mouths. But I lost the two biggest barbel I ever hooked, one through ineptitude and the other through a poor hook hold, the latter being the tragic exception to the norm. I will confine myself to describing my incompetence; it has, after all, become familiar subject matter in this chapter.

The scene was again Naburn Locks on the Yorkshire Ouse. I had now passed my driving test and had borrowed Dad's car for the night; it was late June, hot and still. The river smelt gorgeous in a tidal, muddy sort of way, and as dusk fell I started to get a succession of bites and hit every one. Eels first, then the odd floun-der and small bream; all on lobworm, the bait which will catch anything, anywhere. And then came a bite which almost pulled the rod from my hand as, somewhere deep in the river, 20 or 30 yards out, a barbel had taken the bait. It rampaged upstream, and the clutch screamed incessantly. I wasn't in control, I didn't know what to do. So I decided – obviously – to tighten the clutch, to show the fish who was in charge. *It* was . . . the bloody line snapped.

Probably not a huge barbel, but bigger than anything I had experienced before. It could even have been a salmon, as in those days there was a reasonable run up the Ouse and I well remember watching an eight-pounder being landed on trotting gear by a stunned matchman. But I hope that it was a barbel – it just would have been more fitting, more meet.

I didn't even hook the biggest barbel I ever saw but I did nearly stand on it. I was fly fishing the Ure in mid-Wensleydale on a golden early summer evening, the time of year when barbel spawn on the shallows. I was fishing for trout with small nymphs, and my mind was focused on sub-surface swirls and the glints of feeding fish – so I crashed through the broken water shallows at the tail of the pool with little thought apart from the prospects upstream, where the pool slowed to nymphing pace. The water in front of my waders was suddenly cleaved by a gigantic barbel, golden brown in the sunlight. Not a very long fish, but almost as deep as a carp. It writhed and thrashed its way into the deeper water above . . . and then I remembered to breathe. It was like seeing a UFO, a brief glimpse into the unknown and unknowable. I suspect the fish weighed perhaps 12lbs, perhaps more; not a big fish now, but enormous for Yorkshire in the early 1980s.

Fishing is so full of contradictions, ironies, reversals and double meanings. Its language is reliant on nuance, on inflection, even on volume. Losing fish is the most traumatic experience of all; the loss can sear the senses, consume the angler with regret. But would we exchange that despair, so acutely felt and feeling like an immovable weight? Would we exchange it for what could have happened instead? Perhaps, but only if the 'instead' meant the fish had been caught. If the alternative had been a forgotten afternoon on a forgotten venue long ago, I would rather live with the memory of loss. Scars add character to the most forgettable of faces; scars heal but they remind you of the day when you so nearly succeeded. Ludwig Nietzsche said it – 'That which does not kill you makes you stronger.'

CHAPTER FIVE

A Dilettante Salmon Fisherman Writes

*I wonder if we could contrive some magnificent myth that
would in itself carry conviction to our whole community*

Plato, *The Republic*

M**Y LATE FRIEND** J**ON** Stevens often characterised salmon
fishing as the toughest game in town. I was sceptical then
and am no less so now. Of course, it depends upon one's personal
take on just what toughness means. If you take it to mean the need
to spend fruitless hours fishing for fish that are probably not there
and, even if present, are disinclined even to look at fly or lure, then
I would agree, it is a tough game. But I do not think the fishing
itself demands quite the levels of skill that trout fishing can require,
or, indeed, most branches of coarse fishing. I will upset some of
my friends by writing this, and they will quite rightly frown deeply
as they remember my distinctly lightweight approach to salmon
fishing. Especially as it normally involves piggy-backing their
groundwork. But I do have a reaction to the *faux* mystique that
surrounds salmon fishing, and perhaps some discomfort with the
elitism it can be perceived to perpetuate.

I have spent too much time in the bars of Highland hotels listening to nonsense and half-truths spoken about every aspect of salmon fishing. I have heard those tales of mythical rivers, available only to the tiny privileged minority, which produce bounteous quantities of huge springers. Folklore is always entertaining, and this is no exception, but, once removed from the hysteria in which fishing folk fired up on good whisky can indulge, ten minutes' research in *Where to Fish*, or *Trout and Salmon*, or, especially, on the internet, will reveal that actually, and prosaically, those exclusive rivers are often accessible for the price of a phone call and a modest cheque. Or they haven't fished well since 1978. Or both. And then there is the whole catalogue of reasons as to why the fish are not being caught. Too hot, too cold, too bright, too dull. River running too high or too low. Air temperature rising. Or falling. Water temperature ditto. Fish running through. Wrong time of day. Bad year. Poaching. Unexplained influx of polluted water into river, covered up by the authorities. Face it, salmon fishing can seem a conspiracy theorist's playground. There is a reason – actually two – why salmon are not being caught. Firstly because they are not there or, if present, they are there in such small numbers as to make fishing for them a lottery. Or, secondly, because many salmon fishermen could not catch the proverbial cold. I have rarely seen such incompetence, nor more widespread, than on my occasional days after the silver tourists, as Chris Yates so memorably termed them. Hopeless tackle, clod-hopping ineptitude and a lack of basic watercraft. A good coarse or trout fisherman would put many of these amateurs to shame.

As would, of course, a good salmon fisherman. And I have met some of those too; they are the type of people who practise what they preach; if you are fishing for salmon the secret involves something really quite tedious. Like ensuring that your fly or spinner is in the water for most of the day, rather than hooked in your keeper ring as you pontificate and bluster about why the fish are not co-operating. And, when I read about the bounty that the rivers in Alaska or Russia can produce, I do not think that the fish there are any more stupid or co-operative than ours. I do not think the conditions are any easier than on our domestic rivers. The helicopters and the vodka may add a superficial glister of glamour but essentially it is the same set of problems. Except – out there – there are just more salmon and shorter odds, OK?

End of jaundiced introduction. This is where I peer from my slit trench to see if it is safe to emerge, or whether the fusillades of the Tayside Guards or the Oykel Grenadiers are still whizzing overhead. The truth is, I find salmon fishing a lovely way to spend the day. And I mean that in a quite literal sense, as it is truly the only form of fishing which I can enjoy without having any high expectation of actually catching anything. I have never subscribed to that loser's philosophy about mere presence at the waterside being sufficient, of how any fish is a bonus, as if a gift from God, because it is nonsense. I fish because I want to feel a fish smacking the rod tip round, want to hear the reel scream, want to feel the cool weight of a fish in my hands. But I do enjoy my days with a double-handed rod, searching the pools with an Ally's Shrimp or a Willy Gunn, feeling the satisfying heft of the long rod, the almost animate feel of carbon under load from 15 or 20 yards of fly line. And I love the shape of the fly line as it arrows across the river, or is confused into doing the impossible with a double Spey. Even the noise can appeal – there is an irresistibly macho element to that whippy hiss of the line as it flays the scenery above you.

Another confession: despite my over-developed scepticism on some aspects of salmon fishing, there are few experiences in angling which even begin to compare with that electric jolt you feel when you know, without doubt, without reservation, that you – yes, you – are hooked into the wildest fish of them all. Not necessarily the wildest in the sense of the hardest fighting but the wildest because of what salmon are, where they have come from and what they do. The few I have caught pulled hard and fast, although I am the last person to pass definitive judgment. But, as it is my book, I will anyway; I suggest that a fit pike, carp or barbel of equivalent size, hooked on the same tackle and in the same current would fight just as hard. Chippy? Perhaps, but maybe I just resent the dogma that can infect what is a truly noble branch of the sport. The point is that salmon fishing should be part of fishing's broad church, not a separate religion whose believers practice a zealot's intolerance of other faiths. But, as a friend put it, salmon fishing can be an addictive game – David characterises it as the heroin to trout fishing's marijuana. Which makes bream fishing what, exactly? A decaffeinated latte?

Let me tell you now about my first salmon. Jon had pushed and cajoled me into diversifying from my menu of carp, chub, barbel and trout. He had finally persuaded me to try a week's salmon fishing in Scotland. Jon did not do many things by half measure and so, despite my complete lack of experience (and, I suspect, not quite as much experience on his part as Jon's Olympian self-confidence might have suggested), we booked a week on the Tay. Not, in hindsight, a river for the inexperienced nor the faint-hearted. We fished at Dalguise, where a forty-something-pounder had been caught the previous season. We stayed at the Grandtully Hotel, and when being driven down to the river by mine host – who, obviously, was an Irishman called Scott – my vocabulary was sternly corrected and I was instructed that a trout was a trout, but a salmon (and only a salmon) was a Fish. Which is a piscatorial counterpoint to Kipling's comment that a woman was only a woman, but a good cigar was a smoke. And how much simpler my life would have been had this only been true . . .

I had never experienced the delights of a fishing hut before, nor the need to be introduced formally to one's fellow anglers. They seemed a decent crew, ranging from the retired Colonel and his wife – barking but charming – to the trio of Edinburgh police inspectors whose main priority was to empty their daily 40-ounce bottle of Famous Grouse. (They reminded me, in a knitted-brow display of tongue-in-cheek machismo, how I 'would nae get pissed on that, laddie' as they guffawed at my lunchtime Diet Coke.)

Mike Smith, the owner-cum-ghillie, reminded me of the etiquette of actually fishing a pool – cast, take a step downstream, cast again. And, of course, let the gentleman with the fly run through a pool before it is violated by the prole with the spinner or the hodge with the worm. It was just a pity that Mike was unable to speak to more Scots salmon fishermen on this point – they might have learnt something which would have improved the quality of visitors' sport.

I had bought a double-handed rod for the holiday – at some price, as I had part-exchanged two beloved carp rods for it. The rod was a brown North Western 12-foot glass thing, and was hopeless – too short, too heavy and utterly unsuitable for the Tay. My complete lack of experience, and hence technique, in fishing a double-hander, was no help either. With the arrogance of youth (I was twenty-six), I had assumed that, because I could bash out 25 yards of line with a decent double haul on the banks of Rutland, casting a double-handed rod over a similar range would be a formality. One hand good, two hands better, obviously; but I could not believe how difficult it actually was. I hadn't realised the difference in technique, in both timing and execution. It felt like left-foot braking, left-handed writing or walking blindfolded: impossible, alien and clumsy. And it felt like a performance whose only purpose was its practice; it was a means with no credible end.

The Tay was fearfully . . . big. And fast. The current was unbelievably powerful, and just wading a few yards out could feel like a potentially life-changing decision. The river wasn't all shallows either, as just in front of the fishing hut the pool looked almost bottomless. But it was a simply joyous experience to fish this big, beautiful river in early June. There were wild flowers everywhere, a hundred different greens on the riverbanks, and I experienced a feeling of near rapture at the bounty of it all. Deer were a common sight in the woodland in the upper reaches of the beat, and if I had seen a grizzly or an elk I would just have accepted it as part of this paradise. Concrete bowls have never looked the same since.

We saw Fish – note the capital F – often, and we heard them too. They were silver, huge and so exotic as to seem quite unattainable. I could not even admit the possibility of acquaintance with these creatures, because clearly they lived in a world different to my own. Imagine you are next to the catwalk at Milan Fashion Week – covet, lust over Kate Moss, but accept, with a leaden certainty, that she is never going to be your new best friend, let alone your significant other. That's how salmon fishing can make you feel – out of your depth, not even a convincing impostor. But even being a spectator felt almost enough as we fished – hard – on this most spectacular river. On the afternoon of the second day, whilst fishing from the far bank through a fast nearside run, something hit my Devon minnow with venom. (I had abandoned the double-hander after the first day). Of course, it had to be a salmon, and it certainly pulled tough and fast, but they don't make salmon that small, usually. It was a 2½lb sea trout, silver bright and with a body that felt impossibly taut after the flabby rainbows I usually caught.

That evening Jon caught a big grayling on his fly rod and later, and extraordinarily, an eel on a Devon. We fished on, day after day . . . and, for once, just being there was almost enough. We met up with the people who had taken the beat above, Kinnaird, and they told us they were going home early because sport was slower than expected. God knows what the water had cost them for the week – Kinnaird is not in the Poundstretcher class. We were invited to fish the beat if we wished; I did wish, and on the last morning of the holiday walked up through the woodland to the lower pools on Kinnaird. The water seemed streamier, more accessible, and even with my tyro's eyes I knew it was better salmon water and much more suited to the fly. But I stuck with my spinner and I fished down the pool with my cut-price Woolworths Toby – I think rebranded as a Winfield Shanny. I had been warned against using Tobies, as they were poor hookers, but I had taken the suggested precaution of adding another treble to the top split ring. By this stage in the week, my casting was near perfect, and I was able to drop the lure to within a foot of the far bank every time. Most of my tackle was suitable but the line was the embarrassing exception. It was a little short of what was required; but it was that specimen-hunter arrogance – I knew that I could stop anything that swam in my local gravel pit on 12lb line, so why should I kowtow to the game-fishing mafia's suggestion of something much stronger? The reason was clear as soon as I had seen the breadth and pace of the Tay and the size of its occupants, and I had cannibalised a spool of 15lb line I had brought with me for making leaders for the fly line. Unfortunately there was only 30 yards left, but my blood knots were reliable so why worry? Why indeed?

If you have read enough fishing literature, you will be aware of the fact that some anglers occasionally experience premonitions. Not in the relatively common context of finding oneself playing a fish, having struck at something imperceptible, which you perceived by sixth sense, but in a much more profound way. It has happened to me on three or four occasions, and it happened to me on that day in 1979 on the Tay. As I was casting, I knew a salmon would take the lure. 'Know' is a lightweight, commonplace word, but in this context it meant absolute conviction: cast-iron certainty, total inevitability. It didn't even manifest itself in this dramatic style – I was just aware that this is what would happen. It did not feel odd or spooky – why should it? It felt as straightforward as knowing you will be drenched by the fast-approaching curtain of rain being wind-driven towards you.

So there was no surprise, if no preparation either, for what did happen. You might expect a description will follow of a great swirling boil at the lure, or a lunging dive at the rod tip. But the reality was really quite curious. In the fast water at the head of the pool the mere action of the lure was enough to apply pressure to the rod tip, quite significantly so. And suddenly all the pressure was released and the line slackened, was pulled taut and slackened again before I lifted into something which felt bigger than I had dared hope for. There were no leaps but there were sullen, authoritative runs down the pool. They were unstoppably powerful, and I followed – this was one of the few pools where there were no trees or obstructions to hinder progress – and I covered 60 or 70 yards before the fish slowed and started to circle, making huge swirls in the mirrored surface. The salmon made progressively shorter runs, but not so short as to remove that ghastly reminder of my lack of preparation when the blood knot clicked over the rod rings time and again. Eventually I saw her, and she was enormous. I did have a tailer, but in the excitement had left it on the bank many yards upstream. I had read about hand tailing – possible with a salmon but not with a sea trout – so I grabbed her by the wrist of the tail, stumbled through the shallows and fell on the pebbled bank, salmon beneath me.

She weighed 20lbs and was silvered perfection. Stunned, elated, walking on air, I carried her back to the hut; I saw Jon who was overjoyed at my success. Far more so than if the roles had been reversed, I will admit. I was fêted in the hut by the policemen. They succeeded in persuading me to abandon the Coke for the Famous Grouse, even though I had caught, as they put it, 'a fucking kelt'. Yes, a fresh-run kelt at that, oh green-eyed monsters! I was fêted in the hotel too – as soon as everybody heard I had caught my first Fish drinks appeared from nowhere. From the local forestry worker to the tweeded gent in the corner – who up until then had not admitted I occupied the same room – everybody was my new friend. And it was truly wonderful.

Since then I have played around at salmon fishing. Fished the Tees for three seasons, saw the fish, covered them, but hardly a take. Lost one on a Czech nymph on a bone-cold December afternoon; it was the briefest of acquaintances but it was contact. Believe me, Tees fish are as rare as they are big. I tried the Wear but was put off by the burning Rover 214 on the riverbank and the feral locals who ferreted along the banks. Did the North Tyne for a year – or, as it turned out, three days, as time was hard to find. Lame excuse: I really couldn't be arsed to do a 200-mile round trip probably to catch nothing when I had superb wild trout fishing almost literally on my doorstep.

I have fished for Scottish salmon again though, and even caught a couple. I lost a fish on the River Garvie in Wester Ross, running north out of Loch Osgaig into Enard Bay, a short mile away. Our beat had one long pool and lots of fast pocket water full of tiny sea trout. But the big pool had salmon at home, and they crashed and wallowed in the weedy margins. Stupidly, I was fishing a lightweight rod with a 6lb leader; well frayed by contact with the rocks in the faster upstream reaches. I fished my fly through the entrance to the big pool; the line stopped; there was a salmon-sized heave on the line, and it snapped. Another brief encounter.

I had more success on the Nith, thanks to Frank the Ghillie and Neil, my friend. Neil is a tough fisherman, he doesn't agonise about whether he should be fishing in bad conditions, doesn't vacillate between hut and lounge bar, he just goes for his week and he fishes solidly. And Neil catches, too, especially on worm, at which he has become a master. His technique I found quite compelling to watch, so unexpected was it in its execution. I had imagined a lazy variation on legering for barbel, rather than this short-range exploration of every contour of rock and boulder, which demanded concentration, technique and a determination which this dilettante lacks.

And the salmon which in many ways I value the most is the fish I caught on the Nith in 2003. It was a bitter cold autumn morning and as we walked down over hard-frosted fields, the Highland cattle exhaled huge plumes of condensation in the stillness. As ever, the dippers were busy on the river, and even the odd salmon was rolling in the mill pool, despite the cold. The pool was in shadow, and therefore even colder. Neil suggested that a Rapala or a Flying Condom would be the method, and, whilst I did not doubt him, the aesthetics of the double-hander were too strong an attraction. And the rod has its own history. It's a Bruce and Walker 14-foot salmon rod that was lent to me in 1999 by Jon, who died in a Highland car crash in August 2000. Tragedy transformed loan into bequest, and the rod needed to be exercised. The mill pool is easy fishing compared to the challenges of the Spey or the Tay; it's not too far to cast, and there is reasonable room behind you if you cannot execute a double or single Spey. (And I prefer the double – purely on aesthetic grounds; it just looks so damn good.) Bizarrely, unexpectedly, I was playing a fish within five minutes of starting. Neil was amazed, I was delirious, and only the salmon was less than ecstatic. It wasn't a big fish, at 6lbs, but it was one that had a resonance far beyond its weight. I have toasted friends with whisky before but never with a fly-caught salmon.

CHAPTER SIX

ESOX AND I

Thou hast no speculation in those eyes
which thou dost glare with

WILLIAM SHAKESPEARE, *Macbeth*

T HE LAST PIKE I caught weighed 12lbs and the bastard broke
my landing net. In these politically correct times, when to be
less than fully prepared for the deified species of carp, pike and
barbel is akin to heresy, perhaps an explanation is needed. Or at
least an excuse. It was late December and a mild afternoon; I was
fishing the Swale for chub, and because of the blue bright sky I
had not had a bite until 3.50 p.m. when the light started to dim. I
experienced the familiar and welcome sight of the quivertip knock-
ing abruptly twice before curving round to the pull of a fish. A
chub of about 3lbs with a weakness for Danish Blue cheese paste.
I know the rules of this game and I threw in more mashed bread,
recast and at 3.55 p.m. I had the next entirely predictable chub
bite. The fight was chub-like too, with deep lunges towards bankside bushes and a bull-headed determination to keep away from
the net. The scale of the fight was, however, completely outside
my experience. It fought like a chub, but even five-pounders did
not pull that hard. This fish had to be six-plus or (whisper it) even
a seven. And the big question is – why did this gigantic chub

transform itself into the only vegetarian pike in the whole bloody river? I have caught hundreds of chub on this bait and, until now, only two other species. One of each: an equally unlikely grayling (curiously enough from the same stretch of the Swale) and a silly escapee rainbow trout.

So my relationship with pike has never been on a very solid footing. But you don't need to be an item to have fun – you can be in the relationship for what you want to get out of it without all that guilt stuff. This is probably why I fish for pike – I do it for kicks. I have never thought of any aspect of my fishing being comparable to one-night stands but I am starting to wonder about it where pike are concerned. I am told it can be a lot of fun but it can never become a way of life – or at least it shouldn't.

I will confess to an element of an apprehension each time a pike float surges beneath the surface of the water – not for the fight to come but for the rather messy business of landing and unhooking the fish. They are very big, they have sharp teeth and despite one's best efforts, are sometimes firmly hooked in a position which necessitates minor surgery. These are the times when I much prefer a docile chub or barbel with their soft mouths and a reassuring passivity once on the bank. But pike get angry, they stay angry, they thrash about and they are past masters at impaling the temporarily forgotten set of trebles in net, hand or wader. The thought police will even now be frothing with righteous indignation at the fact that this bumbling amateur of an angler sometimes struggles a bit with pike; I may be offered a teach-in, or perhaps some re-education to follow the group criticism.

A little bile is starting to seep into the text, I admit. Trouble is, I can rarely approve of single-issue pressure groups, especially when they attempt to impose their own moral framework upon others. Hypocrite, *moi*? To a degree. I have been a member of the ACA for thirty-five years, and was one of the earliest members of the Wild Trout Trust. But I think that I can draw a distinction between organisations whose sole objective is the preservation and restoration of habitat and those pressure groups of self-appointed moralising guardians with no facility for considering views other than those identical to their own narrow-minded dogma. Nothing wrong in preaching best practice; nothing wrong in encouraging anglers to prepare for their quarry or to respect and preserve it. But I do find it curious – no, ludicrous – that the people who so encourage me to look after my pike as if it were a premature baby are the same ones who continue to support the barbarity of live-baiting. Tell me this – why is the life of a roach, dace or bream somehow inferior to a pike's? How does the live-baiter reconcile his respect for the quarry with his contempt for the bait fish? In an environment where unhooking mats are *de rigueur*, how can it be right to stick a treble hook into a living roach's back? And, as for the practice of releasing unused live baits into waters in which they are not even found naturally . . . I could find the words, I could write a paragraph of coruscating criticism but should I really need to?

So, dear reader, it seems that I may have a problem with both pike and some of those who hunt them. I will own up to both charges, but I can also say that there is very little in angling which can excite more than the first sub-surface jolt of a long-motionless pike float. It is electric, and the experience lasts so much longer than the almost subliminal occurrence of a trout engulfing an upstream nymph, or a dace breathing in a stick-floated maggot hook-bait. And until you have seen a few double-figure pike, you would easily believe that they weigh twice as much, so long are they and so very threatening.

I cannot remember the first pike I caught, but it would have been in one of the ponds around Allerton Bywater, or perhaps at Fairburn Cut, where we had the luxury of a short length of unpolluted canal to fish. Most of the local waters were alive with small roach and a correspondingly large population of small pike. We live-baited – because back then that's what everybody did. And it worked, even though some of the jack pike were barely strong enough fully to submerge the wooden *Fishing Gazette* floats which we used. The pike rarely fought hard, and unhooking them was never a problem because we killed every one we caught – again, as people did then, in the belief that one less pike would mean a hundred or more roach, that pike ate their own weight in fish every day, or that they killed for fun, like a fox. Now we know much more about biomasses and food chains, but I still belong to a fishing club, many of whose members are at a loss to understand not only why I choose to fish for pike in the winter months but that I actually return them unharmed. In parts of North Yorkshire they are still regarded as if they were rats in your kitchen. But I view them as the top guys, big, hard and beautiful; predators strutting around the apex of the pyramid and ready to outstare anyone or anything.

My first memorable pike came from the South Forty Foot Drain in Lincolnshire, a few miles from Boston. It was before I had moved to Lincoln from Yorkshire, and I had travelled with other members of the long-defunct Leeds and District Specimen Group for a weekend in the Fens. We had done our research, read our *Angling Times* and even written to such luminaries as Barry Rickards about where we should fish. We had started the day by fishing with military precision – we fished each (apparently) identical length of the Drain for twenty minutes, then overtook our partner up or downstream (it was often difficult to work out which on the sensorily deprived world that is Fenland). I lasted until lunchtime before losing interest; I had no feel for the species, nor the location, and I cast my sprat aimlessly into the middle of the drain, stuck the rod in the rod rest and chatted to two equally bored specimen hunters.

After discussing the latest Pink Floyd album – *Meddle*, since you ask – smoking too many John Player Specials and speculating about barbel prospects in the summer, we fell into the reverie so familiar to fishermen who have spent a lot of time with each other. Nothing has to be said at all, but if anything should be said, then this is a good time to do it. Then the rod-tip tapped. The rod was a 10-foot Avon Fibatube, more accustomed to semaphoring the rapping take of a Wharfe chub or an Ouse barbel. The bite here was similar, perhaps a little more leisurely but with that urgency, that insistency that is impossible accurately to describe, but equally impossible to mistake for anything else. I lifted into a solid weight, which then swam slowly across the drain. The line was already flagged with weed, and the pike was soon crowned with the stuff. An unsighted pike does not fight with conviction or intelligence, and I pulled her over the waiting net and marvelled at the creaminess of her belly and her yellow-flecked green flanks. Of course, she was enormous, and our trio of tyros did not even dare to guess what she might weigh. The scales were produced and – I admit it – we had to double- and treble-check that the pike was actually 13lb 6ozs and not the 23lb 6ozs that would have been so plausible, had the indicator on the scale only moved into the next colour graduation. There is a picture of me and the pike in my album. I have long hair, I am wearing Buddy Holly glasses (actually nothing like as cool as Buddy Holly – think Hank Marvin instead); I am also wearing, bizarrely and unaccountably, a Blizzard ski hat to complement my PVC car coat. Strange times, the early seventies.

Loch Lomond appeared next on my pike-fishing radar. It was becoming a very sexy place to fish, and the wild men of the Coventry Circus Specimen Group, as well as their more stable counterparts in the Witham Valley Specimen Group (of whom, now a Lincoln resident, I was a member), had trail-blazed their way north. In spring 1976 we fished Ardlui, although, if challenged, we would have spouted some nonsense about exploring the remote eastern bank of Lomond, as *Angling Times* sensationally termed it at the time – as if it were one of the remoter provinces of Turkmenistan, rather than half a mile from the Ardlui Hotel.

Our trip there was arduous in my overloaded and hideously underpowered 1100cc Ford Escort van. Across the flatlands of the Solway the van had been blown from one carriageway to another like a discarded carrier bag. And our first view of the Loch did not increase that confidence; we had read that tiresome cliché 'inland sea' so many times in the fishing press, often applied to any still-water where you couldn't recognise your mate on the far bank. But Lomond really was an inland sea. It was enormous, it intimidated and was utterly bewildering. Ardlui, with its pleasantly secluded bay, felt like an ideal location to us; even though, in truth, we were paddling in the shallows but convincing ourselves that we were really Out There, surfing the Big One.

Neil, Richard and I fished for a week, and we struggled; we caught three or four pike, all in single figures. Neil lost a double-figure pike at the net and was near inconsolable. The holiday was unproductive but it lit the flame for future trips to what we then thought of as being the real Highlands. The next season we returned, in greater numbers, but to the same location, and we caught pike to 20lbs, with my personal best being a long, lean hunter of a fish of 16lbs 12ozs.

But the truth was, I never developed a real feel, never was able to adopt any intuitive approach to stillwater pike fishing. I would hurl out my dead-baits, play with the bite indicators, daydream for thirty minutes and recast. Aimlessly. What I enjoyed most about Loch Lomond was the scenery, the company and the peripherals. Like spending a light-hearted day catching dozens of perch at Balmaha; like rowing down the mirrored Loch on a still May evening, watching the stags on the skyline and listening to the cuckoos in the glen. Or watching the echo sounder click round to two, three hundred feet beneath the boat as we glided into the main body of the Loch. Or being marooned on an islet at Luss in a sudden squall. It is the very lack of activity in pike fishing – at least in the lazy, undisciplined way in which I practise it – that can make it feel like a life sentence.

But I discovered just how exciting pike fishing can be when I started to fish the River Ure, where I had joined a syndicate just above Ripon, run by Brian Morland. There were 4 or 5 miles of river, I suppose, and the place felt like – was – as close to wilderness as is possible in lowland England. The Ure had long, rocky, fast-running pools, alive with dace and grayling; it had slow, deep eddies adjacent to the pools; and it had one long, slow stretch of 500 yards or more, which had been dredged for gravel a couple of decades previously. The river had a reputation for producing big pike – but where doesn't? – though I had seen little sign of them. Again, this is entirely characteristic of pike, which populate a river like fifth columnists. They are stealth fish, and sometimes they seem simply to materialise out of the river itself. You just suddenly become aware of a long dark green shape in the margins, masquerading as a weed bed or a waterlogged branch. Then you realise it is breathing, alive, and that it is glaring at something with cold intent; the pectorals fan and the whole fish becomes bowstring taut before the tail lashes, there is a cloud of silt and debris and the image reverts to the illusion you suspect it always was. Did I really see that? Was the fish as big as I thought it was?

On a raw cold east-wind day in early 1986 I had driven down to the Ure with pike my quarry – for the first time ever on the river. I fished with one rod only, an 11-foot through-action glass carp rod, which, although originally bought for barbel, has since accounted for scores of pike and carp. It is the perfect soft but steely weapon needed for close-range work with big fish. I set up a float leger rig, with the sliding float stopped four feet overdepth. (Did the last couple of sentences sound a bit odd? A little uncharacteristic? I thought I had better throw in some technical detail to add authority, credibility, but I confess I am really not very good at it. Not too many more technicals in this book, agreed?)

I cast the half-grayling hook bait 5 yards out into 12 feet of water at the edge of the main flow, which had been diverted towards midstream by a line of bushes above me. There was old snow on the ground, tired and grey, and the river was running hard but clear, still fining down from a New Year flood.

I was so out of practice at pike fishing that I had no real perception, no understanding, of the conditions or the location. Both felt OK, in a hazy sort of way, although I suspect I had seen them through the eyes of a winter chub angler. But I waited less than twenty minutes before the float jiggled, dipped and resurfaced. It then resumed its lifeless, rhythmic swaying in the current until a harder, more assertive stab dragged it under the surface and the line was pulled with an audible snap from the clip on the rod butt. Wind down – hard – and lift into ponderous weight. Such a good feeling, and my first Ure pike was landed a couple of minutes later; just over 11lbs. I started to feel confident, to understand just where other pike might be. It felt like osmosis more than intelligence, but it worked: two more pike followed in the next hour. One was an eight-pounder and the other a little smaller. Inevitably, BB's words came to me – 'rare sport this'.

Then I moved a hundred yards upstream to the run-in to the deep section. Here the current pushed hard downstream but gradually lost momentum as the depth dropped away to 15 feet and the river broadened from 20 yards to nearer 35. There was still a tongue of current mid-river and a long crease bisecting the flow diagonally, almost meeting the bankside willows to my right. For a perfect chub swim, it suddenly looked pretty attractive from a predator's viewpoint. I knew there were shoals of dace here and huge numbers of grayling too. Easy pickings, I thought, for a big pike.

It may have been a product of confidence rather than reason, but within two or three minutes of casting the dead-bait – grayling again – into the edge of the crease, the float stuttered away into the main current without any preliminary dips or quivers. When I struck I knew it was a very much bigger pike than the fish I had caught earlier that day. And, short seconds later I knew it was much bigger than any I had ever caught anywhere. It was a long, tough scrap, and the first glimpse of the pike in that leaden January light felt like looking at a crocodile: long, thick as a log and with a broad aggressive head. Landing her was a struggle, but on the bank she was docile enough. She weighed 20lbs 7ozs, I think (because she was actually weighed by a fellow angler, who called '27', which I took to mean pounds and ounces). Looking at the photo now I think that ounces didn't feature in this equation. And, if I am right, I think I caught the same fish again a couple of seasons later on a warm September morning in the same pool. I remember a twelve-minute – and yes, I did time it – arm-aching fight and my best ever pike of 28lbs 10ozs.

But the numbers aren't really important – it's the context in which they were caught. I managed several other twenty-pounders, though I have only the vaguest recollection of the circumstances of their capture. But I can remember some other, much smaller fish, with absolute clarity, such as the twelve-pounder which bow-waved 10 yards over gravelled, fast-running shallows to chase and then engulf a plug. Pike fight much better in the summer months, and this one tail-walked like a marlin, ran like a bonefish. I found lots of hidden slacks and eddies on the Ure, often only a foot or so deep but curtained by willows and camouflaged by weed. They were private, forgotten corners, ignored by most anglers and therefore precisely the type of environment in which pike thrive. And most of the slacks did hold pike, and some of them would grab the plug under the rod top as it was lifted from the surface. It was hugely exciting sport, even if the fish rarely made double figures.

On the right tackle they fought hard and well; and when they appeared out of nowhere, jaws gaping and tail thrashing, you felt you were playing the Richard Dreyfuss part in *Jaws*.

Dead-baiting is pike fishing's equivalent to Wagner – some wonderful moments but some terrible half hours. But plug fishing is the music hall of pike fishing and fly fishing – perhaps a hint of Gilbert and Sullivan? I have yet to manage a big pike on a fly but I tussled with one on the Swale a couple of seasons ago. It took a marabou streamer and, slowly but unstoppably, emptied the fly reel of line and backing until she halted 60 yards downstream and kited into a willow tree. The leader broke, as did the Orvis rod the next time I used it. Maybe they don't have big pike in Colorado?

CHAPTER SEVEN

THE FISH-SHAPED FISH

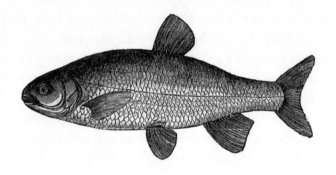

Shall we fight or shall we fly?

ALFRED, LORD TENNYSON, 'The Revenge'

H AS MY CAREER BEEN a success? Well, for a lawyer, I make a pretty good trout fisherman. I read law at the University of Leeds and, in Freshers' Week, autumn 1971, I joined various societies, though I only became an active member of Angling Soc – or LUUAS, as it was known by the Union hierarchy. It is almost too obvious a point to make that at some point in the nineties LUUAS must have become a victim of Students for the Ethical Treatment of Creatures (that we never knew existed until we got to college and felt messianic about something) Society. But the seventies were a lot more laid back, liberal and tolerant. We received a grant from the Union and spent it on rods, reels and hiring minibuses to take us up to the Ouse, Swale, Wharfe or Nidd; the surplus was spent on Tetley's in time-honoured student style. Winters were harder then, and, apart from a couple of weeks of glory in June, after the exams, Angling Soc specialised in fishing for chub – which we did really rather well. Several members became luminaries in the Chub Study Group in later years, and they all caught some hefty Yorkshire chub. It just took most of us a lot longer than Steve Fox, who assumed near legendary status by landing an enormous chub of 5lb 7ozs from Aldwark Bridge on the Ouse. A twenty-first-century chub-hunter would allow that a chub of this size merits weighing, but would not have been fêted as Steve was; chub were smaller then; a three was a good fish, especially from the Swale, fours made red-letter days in the diary, and fives were the stuff of which dreams were made on.

Stuart Shepherd, the President of Angling Soc when I joined, memorably characterised chub as being fish-shaped fish. A prosaic but shrewd description. They are big enough to need a landing net and fight hard enough to make playing them a skill rather than a game. They are shaped like a kid's drawing of a fish; they are solid, deep and with a sort of non-commissioned-officer stolidity. Big scales, big eyes, big mouth and a huge appetite in all seasons for all prey, dead, live or moribund.

Once, sometimes twice, a week we would drive 30 or 40 miles up to Dunsforth or Aldwark on the Ouse, or Boston Spa or Easedike on the Wharfe. We were all devout students of Walker, Stone and Taylor, and we fished in the manner of our idols. Which rather ignored the fact that the Upper Great Ouse in Northamptonshire had very little in common with the Yorkshire Ouse in winter spate. We always used link legered swanshot, never using bombs; we always fished far-bank bushes, and we always used enormous hooks to present correspondingly gigantic baits. We never fed mashed bread, and only rarely did we touch leger or fish a bobbin or other indicator. Long, whippy quivertips were in fashion, even when hooped double by the raging current. And, as for fishing far-bank bushes . . . we did cast towards them, and we fondly imagined our bait bumping round into the (usually mythical) boat channel adjacent to them. But the unequal struggle of six swanshot against fifteen feet of turbulent Ouse water usually meant that we were fishing some near bank desert of a swim. So most of the time we didn't actually catch very many fish; three or four a day was an event.

But in later years we all learnt how to do it properly; we fished near bank creases, we fed hard with mashed bread, we used bombs when the current dictated it, and we would cover half a dozen swims or more in an afternoon instead of planting ourselves in the one. But back then there was a template to our fishing and we rarely deviated from it.

So I really learnt how to chub fish when I moved to Lincoln in the mid-1970s. My first job coincided with my first car, and, with the help of the Ordnance Survey maps for the area, I searched out those lost rivers which sidle almost anonymously through the near-empty countryside around Lincoln. Witham, Barlings Eau, Bain and Devon (River, not county) became regular haunts – especially the Witham. It's a river which is narrow and twisty as it runs north to Lincoln and wide and straight as it then U-turns and slides back to Boston through Kirkstead and the other bream havens.

The Upper Witham was shallow, clear and weedy. In the early 1960s it had been a much prettier river, my local friends told me, but the stalwarts of the internal drainage boards had exacted their usual revenge against nature's presumptuousness by turning the river into a glorified drainage ditch. But the chub still thrived, and in a completely different habitat to their Yorkshire counterparts. In summer it was a stalking game, crouched double and wriggling through the long grass to spot the shoals of fish lying on the honeyed gravel between the weed beds. The method was usually freelined worm or cheese paste, but on the right day it was the street theatre of floating crust. You know the deal – throw in a few samples, witness a series of elephantine swirls and gulps from the greediest members of the chub shoal, and then follow down with a crust on a Size 4.

The winter months provided much slimmer pickings. Location was vital but so very difficult over miles of almost identically land-scaped river. You had to look hard and close to translate the code of tiny creases and vortices which revealed any deviation from the uniformity of the river's course. Bridges and rushes, too, you clung on to any feature which broke the pattern. At the very least it would give you confidence, and at best the chub shared your perception of where would be a good place to live. Timing was critical; the chub had easy lives in this spate-free river, and they rarely dined before dusk in winter. But the fish were big, by Yorkshire standards, and four-pounders became regular catches. But what I remember most is the almost suburban location of the fishing on parts of the Witham. I was used to driving over miles of country lanes to fish the Yorkshire rivers, and dusk on the Ouse or Wharfe was a descent into near total darkness. On the Witham, a mile or two below Lincoln, the sky would light up with the amber glow of street lights, and crowning the horizon, except during Lent, was the floodlit glory of Lincoln Cathedral, which remains my favourite church.

And you could see the Cathedral from the Bain too, although its image was confined to a tiny silhouette on the western horizon. The Bain is a gorgeous little river: narrow, winding and much more natural than the terraced flat banks of the Witham. And the Bain lies in the great rolling heartland of Lincolnshire – not in the clichéd Fens, nor in the surprisingly hilly Wolds, but in that time-less never-never-land between them. It's an area which has always captivated me in a way that very few other parts of the country can do. North West Scotland does, and so do the North York Moors, near my home, but they are both so scenic, so very beautiful that their appeal is almost too obvious. They are both blessed with model looks, and forgotten Lincolnshire isn't. She is the plain girl who, after a week or two, you can't get out of your head. And after a month you realise that you never will. So you need keener senses to perceive Lincolnshire's appeal but, once on its wavelength, you feel as though you have been admitted to a secret society. There is something much more obviously man-made about Lincolnshire than anywhere else in the country; you know that the Romans dug some of the drains, then the Dutch. Vermuyden's Drain anyone? You are aware of the generations of farmers who have worked the land, lived, loved and died in it. You are aware of the immensity of the sky, especially towards dusk, when you remind yourself that the only thing which man did not create is that fabulous sunset. It is a welcoming environment but gentle, and one where it is possible to be alone but never lonely. It is a hard feeling to describe but, once recognised, it stays with you like the memory of your first kiss. It is a countryside you can almost feel breathe – regularly, slowly and deeply, like the comforting presence of a shire horse in the darkness. And who could not fall for a county with such an extravagance of names – Burton Pedwardine, Whipchicken Fen, Old Bolingbroke and Mavis Enderby are particular delights, as is Aby with Greenfield. Never been there, and suspect it is a Brigadoon village displaced from a Hardy novel.

And so I loved the Bain, and I had wonderful days poaching it; no one seemed to know who controlled the fishing, and I was asked to leave only once – by a vicar who claimed, unconvincingly, that he had stocked the river with trout. If he had, they certainly had no appetite for luncheon meat, worms or bread. But I did catch a lot of chub in the Bain, very few over 3lbs, but their eagerness to feed and the violence of their fight in the shallow pools made up for their size. And it was stalking work again – the mystery is why I did not realise for so long that the perfect technique for me was small-stream trout fishing.

When I returned to Yorkshire I fished for chub on the rivers I had grown up with; some things had changed though – fewer anglers fished the rivers, and the fish had increased in size dramatically. In the early seventies, the average Swale chub would weigh less than 2lbs; twenty years later the average rose to almost

4lbs – small-headed, deep-bodied and much younger fish. Eventually, in the early nineties, I caught my first five-pounder, which scraped over the barrier by a scant half ounce, and more quickly followed, culminating in a fit and fat 5lbs 13oz fish in February 1994. This then remained a personal record, which by 2006 had assumed an aura of unassailability. However, on Christmas Eve 2006 everything changed; a high-pressure system had at last stemmed the flow of endless rain – fat depressions which had left the Swale flowing hard and coloured for weeks – and on a falling river, just before the 4.15 p.m. dusk, I landed a portmanteau of a chub weighing 6lbs 1oz. I am not a demonstrative man but I allowed myself a distinctly transatlantic whoop. Even so, it was not quite as loud as the one I uttered two days later – on Boxing Day – when a huge fish of 6lbs 8oz restored my faith in Christmas. So nowadays I am mainly, but not exclusively, a winter chub man, and my tactics are the predictable combination of mashed bread, frequent changes of swim and bread or cheese bait. Never could be bothered with anything more exotic, as most of the stretches I fish rarely see another angler these days.

Big fish can sometimes be the *sine qua non* of angling pleasure, but if their capture always excites the angler, on occasion the process of capture itself can be as important as *avoirdupois*. I started to write this book to tell you how it feels, what you look back on and what you look forward to doing again. It's not meant to be a Gradgrindian account, and so let me tell you about how to make chub fishing really interesting. It isn't too difficult, but it does require a leap of faith, which involves forgetting most of the dogma about where chub live, where and when they feed and what they eat. The longer you have fished for chub, the more likely it is that you have refined your methods down to a couple of reliable techniques which work well, and at which you can now excel. But this isn't the practice making perfect thing: it's bloody complacency. Admit it. So here's how I woke myself up.

I fish a stretch of the Swale for trout. It's in the middle reaches, and, although our water is fly-only during the trout season, there are times when you want to be on the river but trout are the last thing you really want to fish for. Hot dog-day afternoons in July or August; brassy sun, no cloud cover and low and clear water conditions. You arrive at 2 p.m. and you know that not a trout will move until dusk. So you stalk the banks, polaroided and baseball-capped and you fish-spot. And you see . . . lots of chub. They are spooky – Walton didn't term them the fearfullest of fishes for nothing – but they are curious, busy, bustling. They sail in great shoals in and out of the willow branches, and in the gravel shallows they will sunbathe and sport for hours. They chase the odd minnow, they turn over a few stones to see what lies beneath. But what they are really doing is hanging out, fooling around with their mates in the sun. There is an element of blokeishness, of peer group antics, of competition and boisterousness. If any fish were to utter the words 'who spilled my pint?' you just know it would be some brassy 4lb chub, swaggering like a trailer-trash England supporter, St George's flag on T-shirt and with attitude to spare.

If you don't spook them (that word again – they have that unreal combination of extreme caution and rampant curiosity) these fish are easy to catch, especially with a fly. There are variations on the technique. The more spectacular, but ultimately less fulfilling, is to find a school of shallow-lying chub, bow-waving with dorsals flapping in the air and cast a marabou streamer into the middle of the shoal. If you cast the fly line over them, or even allow its shadow to fall, you will create an explosion of scared chub rushing for the safety of the nearest deep water. But if you don't, if you can let the lure plop audibly into the middle of the shoal, you will see first one, then three, then a whole shoal's worth of fins thrusting after the lure as you strip it back towards you. Sometimes the fish will see you and they will melt away before they dare take.

But usually the braver fish (and they are usually the bigger ones) will slam into the lure like something much more exotic – small-mouthed bass perhaps? And they do fight; on a No. 4 or 5 line and a 9-foot fly rod, you will have an entertaining two or three minutes before those silver and gold flanks slide over your suddenly under-sized net. And the chub will look at you like a gormless teenager as you unhook and return it. What did I do? Not me guv, honest. Repeat process until the shoal finally loses interest. How effective can this method be? One of my more hectic afternoons saw me catch seven chub in less than twenty minutes and most of them were over 3lbs.

The even more effective fly-fishing method, because it doesn't spook fish unless you screw up completely, is to stalk fish with a dry fly. Old hands and older books will tell you to use a Zulu or anything big and bushy, and, whilst this works (especially with something sexy-looking like a Hopper), patterns such as relatively small Klinkhamers are just as effective. Chub are such nosy buggers that they will inspect critically every mote, morsel and nondescript which floats above them. They are opportunists and will often take a fly just to see if they like the taste of it. And they can do this with a lightness of touch, a delicacy which is so at odds with their habitually loutish behaviour. A shoal of chub fired up on crust looks and sounds like a Friday night street fight, but a single chub investigating a tiny drowned beetle has a grace which can surprise. It is the unexpected balletic quality you can see in a big man on a dance floor, whose style transcends his bulk.

One hot August afternoon I was walking slowly on the right bank of the Swale, around a deep, slow corner which looks, and is, a pike hotspot in the winter. But today was a glary-sunned, blue-sky day, with neither breeze nor shading clouds. The bank is clay and mud and the water drops quickly away to six or seven feet a couple of yards out. I hardly need to say that this is not good fly water. Or it isn't usually – but today there was a small shoal of chub hovering about two feet below the surface. Because of the slow current, they faced in every direction; they weren't resting but they were moving in a leisurely way, a single fin-flick propelling them to the surface to mouth whatever appealed. A lure might have taken only one or two before they saw through the deceit, and so I decided to use subtler tactics and tied a Size 14 black parachute fly on to the leader. It was nondescript, but suggestive of a host of insects without replicating any in particular. Within a second or two of the fly landing an alderman of a chub ambled over and breathed in the fly with a rise which was in marked contrast to its bulk. There was a tiny, neat, emphatic circle instead of the engulfing wallop which usually characterises feeding chub. The fish weighed just under 4lbs, as did all but one of the following five fish which fell for the same method in successive casts.

But the real *son et lumière* show happens in the conditions when I have heard the words 'global warming' just once too often before I escape the stifling confinement of the office. I drive to the river, savouring the liberty as I slough off whatever persona I had to adopt today, and marvel at why ever I thought that car air-conditioning was a luxury in Yorkshire, even if a necessity in Phoenix. On one particular July oven of a day the car temperature showed 29.5°C as I bumped over the brown scorched hard banks of a low-flowing Swale. There was a hint of a breath of a southerly, and the sand martins were working low and fast over the river.

Upstream, opposite the line of willows, I could see a hundred yards of disturbance over the shallow gravel flats. Chub, shoals of them ganged up in lollygagging languor, with their dorsal and tail fins waving in the hot air. Ever so slowly, without a bow wave, I waded towards them. I tied on a Size 12 Hopper: the first of a succession of them, as each was soon to be chewed to destruction. I cast over the nearest group and waited five seconds before the fly disappeared; the first chub weighed 4lbs 12oz and fought like a pig with its tail on fire. The second fish fought the same, even used the same tactics – a long hard run upstream and then a diagonal bolt for the sanctuary of the willow roots. That fish weighed a couple of ounces short of 4lbs.

And three hours later I stopped fishing, and I stopped counting too, after thirty-one chub averaging 3lbs. Ninety pounds of fish then; this dry fly deal is not, therefore, a sleight-of-hand smartarse technique indulged in only to prove a point. It is deadly and, more importantly, is as exciting a form of fly fishing as I have experienced.

And so fly fishing works for chub; not as a party trick but as a serious method. It is so much better if you can target the fish individually, there is more of a hunt, more precision in the game. And, I will allow, there can be something rather irritating about catching chub by accident when fly fishing. The trouble is, at their best, they can do a passable imitation of a fit brown trout. And this can raise one's hopes to dangerous levels sometimes. Not because the chub is in any way inferior; it is just that a 2lb brownie equates to a chub of 4lbs plus in the desirability stakes. Early in the season last year, whilst fishing a leaded shrimp into a broken-water, gravelled run, I had a classic brownie take. I played that fish for a very long time, becoming convinced that I had hooked a brown trout of immense size. Until I saw that familiar silver scaled glint in the water and realised what it was. There was a flicker of disappointment at its lack of adipose and spots but I picked him out of the net, weighed him at 4lbs 12oz, then I angled his flanks to catch the light. I confess that I then gave him an avuncular peck on the cheek. I don't normally do blokeish stuff with either friends or fish, but chub can make you behave in strange ways – I would have bought him a drink, but . . .

CHAPTER EIGHT

A CONFESSION OF CARP

This suspense is terrible. I hope it will last.

OSCAR WILDE, *The Importance of Being Earnest*

THE LAST TIME I picked up a carp fishing magazine in the newsagents I did not succeed in suppressing my laughter. The photos did it – identikit pictures of carp-fisher and carp – and I could not help but notice the curious symmetry between captor and captive, as if they had started mutually to evolve towards some ghastly hybrid. Shaven-headed fishermen with no neck but big bellies; mirror carp with vast bloated flanks and expressions of benign indifference. Do you have to look like a steroid-pumped bouncer to carp fish in the twenty-first century, and are carp below 30lbs no longer worthy of reportage? So ubiquitous has the carp become that its currency has been devalued to that of a thirties Reichsmark; at least in the eyes of those anglers who grew up in an age when carp were almost mythical, catchable only by anglers with formidable intellects and matching determination. I may ridicule the current carp scene, but the previous generations of carp fishermen looked just as ludicrous. Carp were near deified, and photographs from the seventies and eighties show fish being cradled like newborn children. But, instead of a triumphant, smiling dad, there would appear a frowning specimen-hunter who would either meet the camera with a joyless glare or, more typically, gaze down at his fish in a pose of meek obeisance, sometimes so extreme that all that remained visible was the top of the fisherman's head. There was a deadly serious, almost puritanical zeal about carp fishing then, and it seemed that displaying pleasure was a weakness, perhaps even a sin. Back then, the term 'pleasure fisherman' was a contemptuous tag applied to those naïve souls who fished for fun. As if.

But carp did cast a long shadow in the 1970s, even if one felt disinclined to fish for them. They were at the apex of coarse fishing in terms of difficulty, availability and status. Carp fishing was the Chekhov to the chub fisherman's Agatha Christie, Kafka to the match fisherman's Ian Fleming. And no one who grew up in the sixties as a fisherman was unaware of Redmire, Dick Walker and his forty-four-pounder; most of us had even seen her – Clarissa, remember? – in London Zoo.

I did not see a carp until I moved to Lincolnshire in the mid seventies; there were carp, allegedly, in a handful of Yorkshire lakes, but I doubt if I met more than a couple of anglers who had even hooked one. But Lincolnshire was very different; when I first moved there I made contact with the local specimen group and through them became friends with some tremendously able fishermen. Mick Brown – not to be confused with his pike fishing namesake – quickly became a close friend; he and his wife, June, looked after me like elder siblings as I struggled up the steep hill of first job, strange town, romantic angst and, less traumatically, the need to catch my first carp. Mick was a searingly bright angler, constantly thinking about what he was doing and why, always experimenting, always combing the left field for an original method or venue. He had fished with Rod Hutchinson for years, and, shamefully, I will admit to having bathed in a little reflected glory because I fished with the man who fished with the man who was, even then, near legendary in carp-fishing circles. Whilst I previously had had no strong wish to catch carp, never having really admitted the possibility, now I was in Lincoln I started to believe that I just might have the opportunity. And I did admit to having been seduced by the writing of Walker, Maurice Ingham, Jack Hilton and the rest of the Redmire cult about the smartest of fish. When I found that Ingham actually worked for the same employer as I did there was a feeling that I really had to dip my toe in the deep water of carp fishing.

I can only too easily imagine Redmire, Beechmere or Swancoote Pool; they would be lost in forgotten valleys, dark and mysterious, mist-curtained and with a silence that was almost a weight. The Lakeside Lido was none of these things, but it was where I caught my first carp. The Lido was on the north Lincolnshire coast and it was a holiday-camp-cum-caravan-park; the lake itself was steep-banked and perhaps 5 acres in extent. It had some shallows, heavily weeded in the summer, but most of the water was deep and appeared featureless to my river fisherman's eyes. Mick took me to the Lido in November on a mild but densely clouded day in 1975; I caught nothing, didn't have a run, didn't have a twitch but Mick caught a succession of small common carp up to 5–6lbs. He was a generous and perceptive man and soon realised how desperate I was to catch the uncatchable. After hitting yet another run, he handed me his rod and allowed me to play the next fish to the net. Not a big fish, the same size as the rest but I was captivated by its appearance and, unexpectedly, by its feel. It was a common carp and its scales had the exquisite delicacy of a Japanese painting. They were symmetrical and a gleaming shade of bronze, darkening to a deep blue on the back. And the feel? Unexpectedly, almost uncomfortably, it felt like human skin, cool and flawless.

There was no closed season in Lincolnshire on still waters, and my 1976 campaign started in early May with a 13lb mirror carp.

The fight was not spectacular but I was almost speechless with joy at catching the dreamed-for fish. We returned regularly throughout that oven-baked summer; there were lazy, long days spent idling in bedchairs and waiting for the bobbin to twitch up to the butt ring and the line to blur off the spool. The Lido was a popular destination that summer, and crowds of holiday-makers would descend upon every fisherman lucky enough to hook a carp. Jostling kids, pensioners and mums with prams: hardly the bucolic idyll of my dreams. The Camp HQ was located only a few yards back from the south bank of the lake, and its battery of loudspeakers would crackle and distort news of the afternoon's attractions in the Lido Club or, later in the evening, order late-fishing anglers to pack up and go home to avoid being barred. It wasn't *Hi-de-Hi* and it wasn't *Colditz*, but it did come uncomfortably close to both.

Our fellow anglers were a motley bunch; apart from our secretive little coterie of specimen hunters, there was a host of characters who also fished for the carp with varying degrees of ability and success. The memory of two of them still shines – Big Game was a holidaying miner from Barnsley who took on his carp as if in a bare-knuckle fight. He would strike in a manner more suited to setting the hook into a fast-moving hard-mouthed tarpon, and sometimes one strike was not enough and he would stumble backwards, striking repeatedly as he went. Carried away by his Hemingway-esque belligerence, he once memorably executed a strike so savage that not only did the line snap with a crack audible 50 yards away, the resulting loss of tension on his hefty fibreglass rod caused him to lose balance and collapse backwards in a swearing heap of indignity. Tinlegs was another regular; in those non-politically correct times he was named thus for the very obvious reason. But his double amputee status did not deter him in the least from his sport, although he did have a problem with the steep bank of the lake. He overcame this easily, though, by removing both legs, hurling them to the lake's edge, sliding down the sandy slope on his backside and then re-attaching them. Gratifyingly, he caught his share of carp – and, true to form, he was yet another Yorkshireman.

In the late 1970s, just before I left Lincoln to move back to Yorkshire, the Trent became a serious venue for carp – the fish thrived in the water which had been warmed by the power stations studding the lower Trent Valley. I fished at Winthorpe, a short drive from Lincoln and immediately felt more confident than ever I had on a still water. I do not read still waters well, and I would spend far too much time pretending I was fishing as I daydreamed the long hours away, lying prone on my bedchair and thinking of anything but fishing. I could never translate the geography of most still waters into anything meaningful, but rivers, even big ones like the Trent, spoke a language I could understand. I employed chub and barbel tactics for the Trent carp, using sweetcorn and meat for bait, and I started to catch carp within twenty minutes of arriving on my first visit. Trent carp fought like barbel, dogged and fast, and the bites would literally pull the rod from the rest into the water. It was easy, blissful sport, and I gorged myself on it in the six weeks before I moved back north. I failed to catch a big Trent carp, but I did land a twenty-pounder for a dazed Sheffield angler who had hooked it on a light swingtip rod; the struggle was epic.

I did not fish for carp again for nearly fifteen years until I investigated a chain of gravel pits a short drive from home; I had heard that they held carp and, more importantly, that these were caught regularly. And I loved the lakes as soon as I saw them; each was of a totally different character, so unlike the uniformity of the typical chain of pits. One was small, cloudy and almost triangular, with a long narrow channel heading up to the next lake in the chain. Another was standard gravel pit fare – indented banks, a couple of islands, lots of obvious features. But the top lake was the jewel. It involved a ten-minute walk, and because of this was only lightly fished; it was perhaps 2 or 3 acres, mainly tree-lined and as clear as water can ever be. One bank had a deep channel running only feet away from the water's edge; another had extensive weeded shallows. With polaroids, carp could be seen cruising the margins, occasionally punctuating their excursions with enormous swirls, whilst other fish could be seen truffling through the shallow water, dorsal fins hanging like damp brown flags above the surface.

Suddenly, carp fishing felt like a worthwhile pursuit again, Unusually for me, I bothered to carry out a little research into the hot baits and methods, and I found that things had changed more than a little since the innocent days of sweetcorn and bacon grill. It was difficult research, as I failed to understand some of the terminology, so out of touch had I become with the coarse fishing scene by then. Feeling uncomfortably Pooteresque, I sought advice from my tackle shop and spent grotesque amounts on sweet-smelling boilies, hair rigs, miniature drills and other stuff I was told I needed. Owning a helicopter rig and a controller made me feel as if I were packing heat, not to be messed with, a contender. I should have known better. If I have one quality as an angler, it is that I can apply an intuitive approach and often make it work. But if I am presented with all the answers, I slavishly follow instructions and invariably fail to catch fish as a consequence. It happened on the pits; after eight successive visits I had seen a lot of carp; they had inspected the boilies in all their manifestations, popped up, nailed to the bottom or floating on the surface. The carp played their role but never quite grasped the plot; they would see the boilie, glide over towards it like brown Zeppelins, inspect it, look towards me with what seemed uncomfortably close to disappointment and then sink back into the depths. I knew what my role should have been in this drama, but there was a communication problem; carp and carp fishermen were behaving like refugees without even a common language.

On my ninth visit I decided to try some intuition; I left my chair at home and the boilies too. Instead I brought a couple of fresh loaves, having decided that, if nothing else, I could at least fish for carp in a manner in which BB and his chums would have approved. I do not say this whimsically; BB had such a profound effect on my approach to the sport that his style demanded a little respect, needed a personal gesture. Think of it as a piscatorial version of the Brighton Run for vintage cars – done because of what it represents rather than what it is.

The August afternoon was stiflingly hot, and the carp were in a languid dog-day mood. Some just hovered, studies in indifference; others cruised the margins, but in the preoccupied, impatient way that characterises fish which will not be diverted into feeding. There were others, though, and they looked much more interested – and interesting. Fifteen carp, perhaps more, were sitting on top of the weed, backs sometimes breaking the water's surface. They moved slowly, if at all, but with a subtlety and a focus which suggested they were curious, alert and intent. And hungry too – the fish were obviously eating something – snails? nymphs? – from the weed, and they were doing so with audible relish.

I suspected that floating crust would be so *passé*, so terribly retro, that the carp would either bolt in disgust or affect an air of disdainful indifference to my cliché of a tactic. Perhaps it would be perceived as knowingly post-modern? I simply had to find out. Most fisherman hate weed, and the banks were overgrown, virgin, where I stalked the basking carp. I saw two fish, 10 yards out, idling on the surface, making the weed twitch and sway as they hunted for food. Their movements were gentle, industrious almost. I overcast the crust by 5 yards and gently drew it back towards the larger of the two fish. With careful positioning on the bank and some manoeuvring of the rod tip I found I was able to move the crust to within a foot of the carp. Gradually, it became aware of the bait's proximity and turned slowly towards it. Minutes passed as it gazed towards the bait; my heart thudded and the sweat ran in long trickles down my face and chest. It was airless, even hotter and ominously silent. I did not move a muscle, other than my eyes. I watched the damselflies dart over the lake and I saw and heard the clattering flight of a dragonfly, looking like something from prehistory. The carp seemed to have infinite patience, or was it prudence, caution?

Slowly the fish moved towards the bait, mouth now extended in a surprised O. The crust disappeared, sucked in by the carp, calmly and confidently. I tightened and struck; a dozen carp bolted for the weeds, and the rest of the shoal made huge bow waves towards the deeper water. And my carp sounded deep into the weedbed, banged around for a minute or two and was landed: 13lbs. After eight trips, eight wasted days, scores of vacant 'rod hours', I had succeeded with a Size 2 hook, a 60p loaf and a little guile.

I moved to the west bank of the lake where the fish had, I hoped, remained undisturbed and, with the sun behind me, I watched for carp through my polaroids. I saw the usual small common carp apparently playing tag with the shoals of roach and small chub; I saw a big mirror carp roll like a gleaming chestnut barrel 30 yards out – much too far for my freelined bait. And then, to my right I saw two mirror carp emerge from the weedbed into the clear water; they swam slowly together, two or three feet below the surface; they were unhurried, and their body language spoke of engagement, enquiry. I cast across towards them. The bread landed 4 yards away, but the bigger fish immediately glided up to the bait, circled it once and rose to the surface, opening and closing its mouth as it did so. Carp fishing in this style offers plenty of foreplay; you see the fish, note its intent, watch its reaction, wait for it to decide what to do; change its mind, reconsider and then, long minutes later, commit. I waited . . . waited . . . until, decisively the carp breathed in the crust and flicked its tail to return to its companions. I struck and the rod juddered round into a fighting curve as the fish bolted back towards the centre of the lake. I was using the same glass barbel rod I had employed for river pike, and it felt like playing a carthorse. After five long minutes I won, and a fish of just under 18lbs lay submissively in the net. Carp fishing suddenly felt almost like trout fishing, but with a distortion of scale and time which made it a much better way of spending a hot summer afternoon than chasing indifferent brownies with an oxygen deficit.

Mystery unlocked, and once again the secret was that there had been no secret. Over the coming weeks I indulged in catching as many carp as possible and, as I had learned on the stillwater trout fisheries of the south (see Chapter Twelve), the more overlooked and overgrown the location, the easier it was to find and catch fish. They loved the hidden corners where they were free from the bombardment of 4-ounce leads and boilies cast by the proper carp fishermen on the odd occasion they dragged themselves away from their bedchairs and serried ranks of identical rods. Perhaps the carp sought out the seclusion to escape the random beeps of malfunctioning buzzers? I know that I did.

One particular corner delighted; it was an area perhaps 70 yards long and 30 wide, with three tiny islands separating the shallow water. Lying on the high bank it was easy to watch the carp appear out of the main lake and idle through the shallows like families of wild boar. Something would always attract their interest, and they would root socially on the bottom, tails waving. The carp would often disappear from view altogether as they ploughed the lake's bed and sent up huge billowing clouds of silt. Casting a crust near these groups of fish was an exercise in patience and deceit. Fish were always quickly aware of the bait, eyeing it up, nosing it suspiciously, inhaling it only immediately to exhale it again before the hook could be set. Other, more determined fish would hover beneath the crust and simply suck the bread in and carry on swimming until arrested by the strike. And playing double-figure carp in 2 feet of water could feel like a circus act, as the fish bolted around islands or grounded themselves on shallow mud banks. And sometimes I fished blind into more open water; and there were days when even the bigger fish seemed to lose all caution. Ideally, there would be a hot southerly breeze with heavy cloud cover, and the wind would blow up a big rolling wave into the tightening bay in the north-east corner. The carp loved to patrol such places and would attack the bait without caution or warning; the water was deeper there, and the fish would accelerate hard and fast towards the main body of the lake. I remember the sounds of this sport as much as the sight and feel of it: rod creaking as it struggled to control a double-figure carp on its first long run; clutch clicks combining to a continuous wheezing scream; and, most of all, the sound of taut nylon singing high in the wind.

When the weather cooled the carp lost interest in floating baits, but I maintained my interest in the carp; I still had no faith in my shop-bought boilies and decided to treat the carp as if they were stillwater barbel. And so I would bait up a margin swim with two pints of hemp and float-fish sausage or meat on top of the loose feed. It was a very different type of sport, but still utterly absorbing; on the clearwater lake I would sit 3 yards back from the water's edge and, after twenty minutes or so, I would stand – so slowly – and check to see if the carp had intercepted the hemp. It was easy to see if they had, as up to six carp would be digging and burrowing the seed from the gravel; I would watch the silt clouds and great fan tails waving slowly as they gorged. I fished heavily over-depth, and bites were usually prefaced by knocks and dips on the float as the fish barged into the line in their hunt for the hemp. When the real take came, the float would disappear as if it was attached to a passing car.

Fishing the cloudy-water lake was very different. At first I was unsure if carp were even present in any numbers, but twenty minutes' observation convinced me that there were enough fish to make it worthwhile. I had seen the occasional swirl out towards the centre of the lake, and the marginal rushes twitched and swayed as the carp sidled between them. Float fishing for these fish again involved setting a hempseed trap and waiting for a patrolling fish to arrive. The water was often only a few feet deep, and, although I could not see them, the fish announced their presence in subtle but unmistakeable ways. Carp displace a significant volume of water, and I quickly came to recognise those tiny swirling vortices, those gentle little flat spots in the ripple, which betrayed their presence. Sometimes it could feel like listening for a whisper, waiting for a ghost, or even anticipating a kiss. It felt as though my concentration, my focus, was responsible for the fish being there at all. It was my first clue that fishing could be about nuance more than statement, faith more than bedrock literality.

My first fish from the cloudy lake was a leather carp of 16lbs whose first run felt as if it would never stop. That fish had the strength and determination of an athlete, and my arms ached when I finally netted her.

I don't fish the lakes at all now. The controlling club carried out a programme of improvement works – the usual oxymoron. Most of the trees and bushes were felled, the banks were planed into brown uniformity, fishing platforms were created, and tracks were made for the lazy fisherman to drive to each lake. Within months of this vandalism, the banks were strewn with more rubbish and detritus than ever before. The last time I visited the top, clearwater lake, I watched a fisherman noisily drive his tired Cavalier to within a yard or two of his chosen swim. He slammed the car door shut, and started to tackle up. Rod rests were hammered in, literally. A bedchair was hurled clattering down the bank. I did not doubt that every carp which had been patrolling the margins had immediately fled to the sanctuary of the far bank. And the most ghastly irony? The idiot fisherman was wearing, for reasons which defy logical explanation, fully camouflaged trousers, jacket and hat. The outfit did, be it said, did stand out rather splendidly against the metallic silver of the Vauxhall.

And the noise from behind me? It was Walker revolving in his grave and BB sobbing in despair. Carp should be a noble fish, and Neanderthal and nobility should never have to coexist; allowing some anglers access to carp fishing seems to me like feeding your pigs on strawberries.

CHAPTER NINE

THE FISHER AT THE
GATES OF DAWN

*When they were able to look once more, the Vision had vanished, and
the air was full of the carol of birds that hailed the dawn*

KENNETH GRAHAME, *The Wind in the Willows*

I INHERITED A GRANDFATHER clock last year, and it sits, slightly
incongruously, in the corner of my kitchen. The house was
built in 1720, and it is reasonable to assume that this is not the
first such clock to live in Holly Tree Cottage. But my clock has a
purely decorative function – apart from during two blink-of-an-
eye moments each day – because it stands, eternally I suspect, at
ten to three. And, if you have read Rupert Brooke, you will be
programmed to repeat those lines from 'The Old Vicarage,
Grantchester':

> Stands the church clock at ten to three?
> And is there honey still for tea?

Two sentences, two rhetorical questions which create visions of a lost generation and a lost England. I am no little Englander; I do not fly St George's flag to show my hatred of foreigners, I do not resent multiculturalism, and I do not care who wins the World Cup either. But there is a part of me which so easily can be seduced by a Thomas Hardy or a Rupert Brooke, charmed and beguiled by their descriptions of a countryside, of church-steepled villages, dusty roads winding between high hedges and mist-covered lakes, hidden in lost corners of forgotten country estates.

This chapter is about tench, the fish that Walton called the physician of fishes. And it is the fish I have always assumed was in Brooke's mind when he wrote his poem 'Heaven', which contains lines which surely could only have been written by a man who knew about his tench. Brooke describes the fishy deity like this:

> And there (they trust) there swimmeth One
> Who swam 'ere rivers were begun,
> Immense, of fishy form and mind,
> Squamous, omnipotent and kind;
> And under that almighty fin,
> The littlest fish may enter in.

Zoomorphism aside, there is something utterly irresistible about tench; their form has a symmetry which delights; their colour is that impossible sheeny combination of brown, green and gold; and, most of all, they manage to convince their captors that, somehow, they do not resent being caught, as long as you look after them properly.

They make you feel that it is nothing personal, that you can just muddle along together in your respective roles of captor and captive. Of course this is all ludicrous anthropomorphism, and I fall into precisely the same trap as those who weep at the death of a rabbit or a badger but are complicit in the barbarity of factory farming by subscribing to the creed that cheap is good.

75

But tench do have a strange effect on me, despite, or most probably because of, the fact that I have caught so few of them. Yorkshire has never been a noted county for tench, and I was too preoccupied with chub and carp in Lincolnshire to exploit its host of pits and lakes for the species. And so most of my tench fishing has been vicarious, seen through the eyes of BB or H.T. Sheringham. The latter wrote, quite unimprovably:

> A cork float with crimson tip is very necessary to proper angling
> for tench . . . it is a satisfying thing to look upon.

and

> The sordid yearning for bites should not be put in the balance
> against artistic effect.

What little tench fishing I have done has been, I admit, a pure act of homage to lines like these. Not only did the time of year have to be early summer, the fishing had to take place at dawn, and the venue had to feel, look and sound as if it were a time-lapsed refugee from Edwardian England. Context was all, and if one key component were found wanting, the whole fantasy would collapse, destroying decades of anticipation as collateral damage.

I knew that if I wanted to catch big tench I should look for some prosaically named gravel pit with the inevitable complement of scrubby silver birch or stunted willows, and with its bivouacked population of anglers talking of bolt rigs and buzzers, Chinese takeaways and lager. I might fish such waters for carp, eels or roach, but tench carried such heavy significance for me that I was prepared to wait until I could play out my fantasy on a stage where disbelief could be suspended, even if only for a few short hours after a misty dawn.

I found my water in the early 1990s, and in every way it was utterly perfect. I live only 20 miles from Ampleforth College, which is often described as the Catholic Eton. The College occupies countryside of extraordinary beauty, nestling against the Howardian Hills and crowned to the north by the escarpment of the North York Moors. And, unusually for North Yorkshire, the area is heavily wooded with deciduous trees. The school's lakes are set in mature, dense woodland a mile south of the main College building. The smaller lake was stocked with trout by the College, and the local branch of the Salmon & Trout Association, of which I was then a member, was regularly invited to fish for trout there early every season.

The purpose of the visit was to capture and release as many stocked trout as possible to ensure that the fish became educated, a little harder to catch. Because, unlike at Bash Street Comprehensive, fly fishing was part of the Ampleforth curriculum. Not sure whether optional or compulsory, but I hope the latter – wouldn't you rather deal with a captain of industry, an Archbishop or an MP who knew his Skues from his Sawyer, his Greenwells from his pheasant tail nymph?

Salmon & Trout Association visits were something of a pantomime; the membership was charming and embraced a diversity of ability; I had unsuccessfully to suppress a smile when the Chairman boomed that he had caught a bloody barbel on his hare's ear nymph. It was, of course, an exquisite baby tench but, as it was not a trout, was not a spotted aristocrat, it could have been literally anything else to our Chairman. And that is how I found out that not only did the main lake have a reputation for good tench fishing, but that it was obtainable for the price of a stamp and a polite letter to the College.

The permit comprised a letter from Brother Gervase, and even if I had never caught a tench, the letter, and more particularly the name of its sender, would have been enough to liven up the between-course ennui of the dullest dinner party.

I love early mornings in summer, when I wake full of hope and optimism for the day ahead; it is almost impossible for it to be too early, as long as there is a growing light in the eastern sky – 'as the morning steals upon the night'.

I woke at 3.30 a.m. on my first Ampleforth day, and the drive to the College was a good overture to a day which met every expectation. The roads were free of cars but heavily trafficked by fur and feather: roe deer leaped in ones and twos over roadside hedges, rabbits and hares did their usual performance of trying to outrun the car before veering under five-bar gates, and pheasants blundered, as if encountering the world for the first time. Even the car seemed to love the early morning, gulping the cold dense air into its engine and feeling faster, smoother than it would on the trip home in mid-morning heat.

I dropped down into Ampleforth Village from the forestry plantations on the edge of the moors and, as I drove through the College entrance, I saw a monk standing outside, head lifted to the rising sun, soaking up its warmth with the sensuality of a cat. We did not acknowledge each other, for dawns like this are too personal to share, too special to allow human encroachment. I drove over the remains of the old railway track – yes, this school had its own station before the War – and parked 20 yards from the lake. I could smell it before I could see it; there was that flat muddy smell of still waters in summer, overlaid by honeysuckle and wild mint.

I walked along the dam and watched the remains of the dawn mist coiling upwards from the far dark corner of the lake and disappearing into nothingness as the mist drifted into the first rays of the sun. A heron flapped lazily away, banking like an old Lancaster bomber over the high beeches. The coot and mallard were awake, too, but contented themselves with quiet mutterings and squawks over by the reed mace beds. As I tackled up, I saw a movement behind me on the dam wall – it was a slow worm, inching its way along the bank behind me on some mysterious task. They are the most inconspicuous and self-effacing of all reptiles, but they are still a delight to encounter.

I mixed the sweet-smelling groundbait – whatever it contained was a far cry from my simple breadcrumb mix in Allerton Bywater days – and the dye stained my hands a deep beetroot red. Laced with sweetcorn and brandlings the groundbait looked and felt irresistible. I plumbed the depth and found 9 feet of water a couple of rod lengths out and I quartered the area with a bombardment of groundbait. I fished a red-topped float – of course – and I cast a few yards beyond the baited area before plunging the rod top beneath the water and retrieving the float to lie over the feed. I had set the float slightly overdepth, and I adjusted it until it was almost submerged by the tension between shotted hook, length and rod tip.

I sat back and beamed the vacant smile of someone with one foot in a fantasy and the other tethered to reality. *This* was what Sheringham had written about the sounds, smells and anticipation of a June dawn. And – how could they have done otherwise? – the tench signalled their arrival exactly as they should have done: here were the needled bubbles piercing through the surface near the float. But there was far more bubbling than I had dare expected as the entire area around the float effervesced spectacularly.

After a few minutes the float swayed; perhaps a line bite. Minutes passed, more bubbling; hand gripped on to the rod butt, ready to strike. A dip at last, pulling the float down to a red dot on the glass-like surface of the lake, then the float surged up out of the water and lay literally at half cock. I struck hard into the fish and the tip of the light match rod was pulled round forcefully as the tench ran for the centre of the lake. I had only ever caught tench before by accident when carp fishing and I was not sure what to expect from the fight – but it certainly was not this. This was much more dogged, determined and powerful. It was not the fast run of the barbel, nor the banzai charge of a hooked carp; it had a much slower pace, but was equally powerful. I was amazed at just how far the fish would run on against the pressure of the rod and clutch. But the fight was straightforward – deep water, no snags and plenty of time saw to that. And the fish was just exquisite as it lay in the net; it was a warm morning already but the lake water was warmer still, and the tench felt, looked, mammalian as it lay in the netting, tiny red eye looking but not seeing in the element which was so alien to it.

I noticed the size of the pectoral fins and I remembered that male tench were the harder fighters. I weighed the fish at just over 3½lbs, placed him in the keep net, recast and in the next glorious two hours caught a further fifteen fish ranging from a little over 2lbs to a little under 4lbs.

It was a morning of such unusual perfection that I felt as though it had been a dream as I drove home in the glaring blue sky heat. Every expectation had been met, even exceeded and for one who was such a stranger to this style of fishing, except vicariously, it felt like having learnt how to play a tune whose melody had haunted me for years. Until now I had always relied on somebody else's artistry to create the tune – but now I could play the dawn solo myself.

Which I did, with sufficient gaps to avoid the tune becoming too familiar – I wanted it always to be fresh, wanted to savour each note, and I confined myself to three or four visits per annum over the next five years. And then, tragically, my ticket was withdrawn on the grounds that the amount of litter at the lake had become unacceptable. Yes, I didn't mention in my description of the perfect first morning that I picked my way through Coke tins, Rizla packets and chip papers on my way to the dam – perhaps they didn't teach good citizenry at the school?

So I haven't been back – but I don't need to – all I need to do is to think of a golden June morning, the smell of red groundbait and the sight of a float being dragged towards the centre of that perfect lake. And, in the winter months, when the light of June seems an impossibility, an historical accident never to recur, when a dawn-misted tench lake seems only ever to have existed in my imagination, I need only to see those hands standing eternally at ten to three to reassure myself that once I had made flesh from fantasy.

CHAPTER TEN

READING, WRITING AND
OTHER STUFF

Say something once, why say it again?

DAVID BYRNE, 'Psycho Killer'

THERE ARE, APPARENTLY, MORE books written about fishing
than about any other sport. It doesn't actually matter if this
is true, doesn't matter if my sport's literature has now been overtaken by a skipful of ghosted football biographies. What I do
know is that men who could write loved this sport, and that their
passion can illuminate the dullest midwinter night. But, ironically,
one of the best books I have ever read about fishing was actually
about football – *Fever Pitch* by Nick Hornby.

Provocative? I would argue that its excellence transcends its
subject matter, in which I have no interest, and because most of
the book's themes share their currency with angling. Because
angling is about hope against expectation too, it's about relived
triumphs and tragedies, and most of all it is about not only what
happened, but how you felt when it did happen. Fishermen and
football fans both love to dissect, discuss and analyse every incident,

and they never want to, never can, quite discard them. And, of course, Hornby writes like an angel; read his work and feel how the words glide from page to page so easily, so fluently, because he is writing about you, about us, about what it is like to feel. His style looks so simple, and the ease of reading suggests that it must be. That is, until you read someone who cannot do it. Where the words have no rhythm, no resonance, no impact beyond the bare shapes on the page. Where the flow is interrupted by sub-clauses leading nowhere, improbable dialogue and leaden attempts at humour often punctuated by the gratuitous exclamation mark!!! Look guys, if it's funny – it just is, it doesn't need the desperate punctuation to signpost it, ok? I am aware of some thin ice I may be stepping on – can I avoid becoming the blackened pot? Two metaphors in one sentence – guilty as charged.

I may earn my living from The Law but neither of us chose each other, it was no love at first sight thing. Instead, we have bumbled along together in a sort of chaste companionship – my pragmatism having long ago overtaken any ambition. It is just something I do, and I studied my LL.B because maths and science both involved languages I could neither comprehend, nor even speak parrot fashion. What, precisely, was the point of calculus, and why was it so important that I learnt about it? Fuck knows – I never worked it out beyond knowing that DX and DY were involved but in what role – pivotal, peripheral, elliptical or funda-mental – I neither knew nor cared. But, if English always delighted, the prospect of being recycled by my teachers into a replica of themselves held little appeal.

And so I scraped my Law Degree, and I spent long years doing conveyancing on autopilot. It was all process, stilted and slow-moving, and it was not an area which encouraged creativity. Eventually I found a niche which felt a bit sharper around the edges, enough at least to keep me awake. Reader, you are spared the details, but I spend my days writing, negotiating and – increasingly – just talking about projects underpinned by buttoned down agreements, studded with terms like 'liability cap' and 'intellectual property rights indemnity. What I really have learnt from my career in the law is that if you use terms like these often enough you suddenly find a compelling need to write a book about fishing.

So the law is an evil, but necessary and sometimes actually rather benign. Because you get to meet some very smart people and, better still, you get those smart people to be grateful to you for enabling their project to happen or their dispute to be resolved. And if you are a Libran, like me, praise is a drug you crave. But, better still, when you are learning the law, you need to read some judgments by Lord Denning. And whilst The All England Law Reports can often induce catatonia, finding a Denning judgment is like finding a sunny clearing in a dark forest (and I'm thinking more Schwarzwald than Epping here). Because Denning was an iconoclast, the champion of the right thing, the just cause, and in his judgments he showed that rare ability to conjure up simplicity out of the complex, and transparency from the impenetrable. His was a verbal alchemy, and he delivered his words in clear, clipped sentences with an economy and a humour which could delight and illuminate. Denning told you the story, as if he were the avuncular don and you the gauche student. (I could identify with that last role, you may not be too surprised to hear. Stephen Fry I was not. Still aren't, actually.) And who but Denning could have started judgments with words like these:

This is a case of a barmaid who was badly bitten by a big dog.

or

It happened on April 19th 1964. It was bluebell time in Kent.

or (my favourite)

Old Peter Beswick was a coal merchant in Eccles, Lancashire. He had no business premises. All he had was a lorry, scales and weights . . . He had had his leg amputated and was not in good health.

The apparent simplicity of passages like these is in inverse proportion both to the facts and to the intellect of the speaker, because, to the less cerebrally gifted, even the simple things can become complicated – Pete Townshend was right all along.

Maybe more judges should write about fishing, because whatever trade is plied by some of the contributors to fishing magazines it certainly doesn't involve too much joined-up writing. And the last spectacularly dreadful piece I encountered was in one of the monthly game magazines. The author is well known, presumably on the grounds of his prowess with rod and camera rather than pen or keyboard, and his subject matter was good enough almost to write itself – it was about fly fishing for huge trout in South America. And the piece was unreadable; it was as though the author had assembled the 300 words which populate most fly fishing articles and programmed his PC to reproduce them in random order, but with an extra side order of typos and !!!s. My dears, it was simply ghastly.

So, far from transcending the subject matter, some writing does not deserve to be applied to my sport. I would like to talk about the people who can do it, especially the ones who, if you have ever tried to write yourself, make you seethe, make you ask those same rhetorical questions about why I did not use that imagery, that metaphor? When I read Bob Dylan's autobiography such questions punctuated every paragraph. The book was a revelation; here was, arguably, the twentieth century's greatest songwriter who celebrates the advent of the twenty-first by producing prose with the rhythm, punch and sheer brilliance of his songs. Dylan doesn't do fishing, but, if he did, even John Gierach's Zen-tinged prose would be shadowed.

Let me go back to my childhood. Again. I had been given various fishing books for Christmas and birthday presents, and nearly all of them described a sport which had little relationship to what I did on my colliery ponds. One relative unaccountably gave me a copy of a slim book called *Fishing for Sea Trout in Tidal Water*, an esoteric subject, even for those who can claim some acquaintance with the species. But a book which had absolutely no relevance to an eleven-year-old marooned, as I was, a hundred miles from the nearest sea trout river. It was well meant, or so one assumes. (As was the present to a friend who knows his Trollope from his Tartt and devours Sterne quickly and comprehensively – doesn't miss the subtext, never lets a reference escape. David is a Jesus College lawyer who wrote two novels for something to do, to pass the time: and they are good books, too, crafted and smart. His poor mother gave him the complete works of Jeffrey Archer. Because? Because her son liked to read. There just are not the words – but perhaps there is some snappy German composite noun from the Schadenfreude School which conveys the yawning chasm which can separate donor from donee.)

I was hungry for angling prose, and I wasn't sated until I was given a copy of BB's *Fisherman's Bedside Book*. In Chapter One I described how Len Grayson was my mentor – and he gave me this book. My copy is a 1946 reprint and 'was produced in complete conformity with authorised economy standards'. Its pages are tiny and wafer thin, but the work punched a long way above its weight. Because it was the first book I had read which made me realise what a broad church I had joined. There was a cornucopia of stories about salmon, trout, barbel and carp, pike and tench, written by a formidable array of contributors, many of whose books I still read and reread.

The first two sentences on the page before the Contents set the tone for the text: lyrical, elegiac almost. They have been known to induce tears in some middle-aged fishermen. Including this one.

Lend me not to another, and I will be a quiet companion in all your wanderings. Wherever thou goest, there go I through the eagle's air and over the wide seas, through heat and cold, calm and tempest, and the changing years.

Later in the same piece he writes:

Ye shall dream of the jewelled fishes . . . of waterfalls, brown burns and the wild lilies.

And so I do, as I suspect does everyone of my generation who encountered this book as a child, when life became an endless series of doors to be opened with important choices to be made beyond each one of them.

In the *Bedside Book* I read of Swancoote Pool, the pseudonymous Warwickshire lake which contained carp of unimaginable proportions, and I read Patrick Chalmers' account of Thames bridges and his glorious description of barbel sporting in summertime:

But best of all I love the barbels because they roll like big brown-and-white cats upon the golden shallows and sing in the moonlight with the *joie de vivre* of June. And because, so, they are all Thames to me and wild rose time and the streams running down from the weir.

Chalmers' book was published in 1932, when he was sixty, and I remain convinced that this passage was a memory of that golden era before the First World War. No one who has seen barbel sport in the shallows in June could fail to smile in recognition at his description.

And was there ever a more perfect piece of prose on the delights of an evening fly fishing than 'The Curved Meadow' by Raymond Hill, a passage which hovers at the back of my mind every time I fish a peaceful trout stream on a drowsy high summer evening.

If you have not read the *Bedside Book* please do so. It is a life-time's joy and delight. It will introduce you to the heavyweights of fishing literature too. Such as?

Try Arthur Ransome; yes the *Swallows and Amazons* guy. He was a professional journalist and it showed. He wrote with an exquisite lightness of touch, and a self-deprecation which never quite could disguise the fact that his fishing career had such an exuberance of variety, such exotic connections. Try H.T. Sheringham as well; if you like *Three Men in a Boat* and you smile at Jerome K. Jerome's Edwardian humour, you will adore Sheringham. His descriptions of encounters with riverside bulls and angry dogs are wry, slow-burning wit, but a century on they have not even begun to tarnish or date.

A man also featured in the *Bedside Book* is Lord Grey of Fallodon. History will record him as Foreign Secretary but anglers will always love him for *Fly Fishing* and ornithologists will remember him for *The Charm of Birds*. *Fly Fishing* is a book which is nakedly personal, almost confessional, and a book which contains the most profoundly moving prose of any text ever written on angling. The context does nothing to alleviate the sadness – the First World War was rumbling on the horizon, and the author was going blind. The last sentence of the book broke my heart, because it has a currency far outside its context. It is about mortality or, more accurately, coming to terms with one's own mortality:

> The time must come to all of us, who live long, when memory is more than prospect. An angler who has reached this stage and reviews the pleasure of life will be grateful and glad that he has been an angler, for he will look back upon days radiant with happiness, peaks and peaks of enjoyment that are not less bright because they are lit in memory by the light of the setting sun.

(Pause for a dram? I think so.)

Ernest Hemingway and John Gierach are also high in my pantheon. I read Hemingway's *Islands in the Stream* during my first term at university and was converted to his spare prose before the end of the first page. He used such simple, straightforward words and packed them into short, punchy sentences. But he created something which could make you believe that you not only could have been there, but in another life you actually had been. His description of an epic battle with a huge blue marlin will never be bettered. He had practised this, of course, in *The Old Man of the Sea*, but the later book is the better. His early work is wonderful too, and *Big Two-Hearted River* epitomises the sheer joyous optimism of time spent on a trout river in wild country.

But the most moving prose Hemingway ever wrote was about neither marlin nor trout, but about Paris and what it was like to be a young man when life still offered endless opportunity. He wrote *A Moveable Feast* in his late middle age, after his own mythology and the paranoia it created had started to consume him. He wrote this about spring, which is the season in which the fly fisherman should savour every bird-songed moment. And Hemingway, with the spectre of old age and death stalking him, writes about when spring nearly failed:

> Part of you died each year when the leaves fell from the trees and their branches were bare against the wind and the cold, wintry light. But you knew there would always be the spring, as you knew the river would flow again after it was frozen. When the cold rains kept on and killed the spring, it was as though a young person had died for no reason.
>
> In those days, though, the spring always came finally but it was frightening that it had nearly failed.

And the saddest words? 'In those days . . .'

And I guess that John Gierach has read a lot of Hemingway too. He has an accessible, fluid and funky style, shot through with a Zen vibe and a uniquely American pace. It feels like an easy ramble on your favourite horse, and if it had a sound it would be that of an edgier, less mannered Garrison Keillor. No one alive writes better about fishing than Gierach – who else could have said, about the attraction which fly fishing gear first had to him

> The stuff fly fishermen carried was both beautiful and serious looking at the same time – like a big jangling ring of keys to a different reality.

I wish I had said that. (I will, Oscar, I will.)

There have not been too many memorable British authors on the sport since the 1950s; there has been no shortage of people writing books, but there has been too much instruction and not enough inspiration for me. My theme in this book is always how it felt, what it was like to be there, and the leaden prose of too many fishing authors has only briefed me on the minutiae of their tactics and tackle. Or has given me a degree of insight into the exact weight of every specimen they have caught with a level of detail which seems a little gratuitous, a little anal perhaps. Fishing is – should be – about passion, not pragmatism; about self-indulgence, not self-congratulation, and about joy, not smugness.

And the photographs – spare me – endless pictures of camouflaged anglers looking down reverently at some gormless carp or barbel which has been caught twenty times before: enough times to be given a silly name that demeans captive and captor. Heather the Leather – there really aren't the words. How I wish somebody would subvert the whole genre and display a line of dead carp on a string or a barbel on a gaff. What sport we could have.

It is not all bad, of course. Chris Yates writes beautifully and with a humour and deftness which is beguiling. You know that, unlike some of his peers, he is writing truly as himself – it is not affectation; the man is an eccentric and should be treasured, if not listed. Brian Clarke writes with an authority and a conviction which makes him almost pre-eminent among angling heavyweights, and Laurence Catlow, bless him, writes with a sensitivity and perception which is as gentle as it is shrewd.

Like many fishermen, I used to be a serial purchaser of magazines on the sport. At my worst, I would devour two weeklies and up to half a dozen monthlies. I cannot describe the relief it was to reduce my consumption; I would buy the things, skim through the first few pages and discard them on the living room table, where they would sit reproachfully in an ever-accumulating pile until I had read them properly . . . or, actually, kidded myself I had done so. I acknowledged I had a problem when I managed to buy the same monthly magazine twice and only realised my Groundhog Day moment towards the end of my cursory glance at the second copy. I realised that I had become a sort of Pavlovian dog figure, conditioned into buying whatever glossy fishing pornography was stacked on the bottom shelves. So I am now much more selective and I actually bother to read the few I do buy with a little more care and attention.

The cracks started to appear for two reasons – the ease of publishing high-quality colour photographs and the increased factionalisation of different disciplines in the sport. I adored *Angling* magazine, and its spiritual predecessors such as *Creel*, because not only was there a huge variety of articles, there was also a density and concentration of text through sheer necessity, as photographs were difficult and expensive to reproduce. And, as any Radio 4 listener will attest, you get much better pictures from words alone. Three thousand words are actually worth far more, carry far more weight than a bookful of high-resolution digital images. I am playing that grumpy old man riff again, a familiar refrain since my fiftieth birthday I will admit, but I suspect I am not the only angler who despairs at the picture/text ratio of about 80:20, if my randomly chosen rag is typical.

But a far greater flaw is the fact that, whilst I do not seek out this month's specialist comics on sea fishing, carp, predators, still-water trout or match fishing, I do have a passing interest in all of them. Ideas should migrate from one discipline to another, as they did when anglers such as Walker, Darling, Bucknall and Gammon deftly brought their skills to branches of the sport which were entirely new to them. Not any more – a carp fisherman (especially a carp fisherman) – can now exist in a bubble devoted entirely to his chosen quarry, and in doing so fail to osmose the developments in other parts of the sport which might help him become a better angler. Frank Zappa memorably said: 'Most rock journalism is people who can't write interviewing people who can't talk for people who can't read'; I guess you can see where I am coming from here, right?

My next reflection in this chapter is, I admit, self-referential and narcissistic. The thing is, writing about fishing as well as reading about it can become nearly as important as actually doing it. I have kept a fishing diary since my early twenties, but most of the text is little more than shorthand bullet points of particular trips. You know the type of thing: '15 May, River Seph; north-east wind; sunny. Saw one mayfly. Fished 11–3. Trout slim but fit. Lost good grayling at net. Ten brownies, to 0-12 and 1 grayling – 1-10.' It's not going to win me the Booker is it?

But I had started to write a little more creatively when I was Secretary of Angling Soc, as previously described in Chapter Seven. We had a notebook in which predecessors had recorded each Club trip, each intervarsity match and every doomed attempt to catch cod from some heaving Whitby coble. It was crisp, factual stuff and never gave any impression of what the day had actually felt like. Did it amuse? Was someone sick on the way home after their first experience of Old Peculier? Did Steve buy a round? Just how many maggots did escape in the hired Cortina? And how many hundred maggots are there to a pint anyway? Did Richard insist (as usual) that he was just starting to get bites as the northerly wind howled down the Ouse at Nun Monkton two hours after sunset? What the hell did that guy Neil think he was doing by catching chub on a swim-feeder – they're for stillwater roach aren't they? And why does Jon insist on turning up forty minutes late every bloody time and then try to charm us into believing that he was doing us a favour by even coming?

All these questions were important, much more important than the answers. And, to the people who were involved, they had much greater relevance and resonance than some emotionless report detailing the first ten places in the match in pounds, ounces and bloody drams. And so I decided to subvert the convention that our record book was for bare reportage by making most of it up, poking fun at those who deserved it and making sure that no one would forget the record of the trip, even if the account was sometimes more than economical with the *actualité*. My technique worked, and as an introverted law student with a serious self-confidence problem I adored the fact that other people – people who were smarter than me, people who had better-looking girlfriends (or, in fact, girlfriends of any description) – could respect me for something I could do and they couldn't. One of my very closest friends, Neil Perry, with whom I have now fished for thirty-five years, joined Angling Soc on my twenty-first birthday. It coincided with an Angling Soc social and my friends had bought me a bottle of Johnny Walker and a bottle of Asti Spumanti to celebrate the Big Day. I downed most of the latter and a quarter of the former before the predictable digestive unpleasantness started. Neil was, he confesses, a little bemused by the unconventional welcome from the Hon Secretary but he holed up in a corner of the Headingley flat and he read the record book, cover to cover. And he was hooked because he got it. And, bless him, he still does.

Reading done, ditto writing. So what is this other stuff? It is that grubby little tributary called politics; it is a watercourse that has always been polluted, and even when it joins the main river its effect can be seen for miles downstream. This stuff takes a lot of dilution. There are some major issues to wade through, princi-pally whether fishing can expect to survive the type of legislation which I suspect is hove to, hull down on the horizon. I have lived through the pantomime which prefaced the banning of hunting with dogs and as I write the first skirmishes are taking place with the lobbying groups who feel that watercourses should be freely accessible to canoeists, using the recent right-to-roam legislation as its terrestrial precedent. And, of course, conveniently ignoring the fact that anglers have no right to fish but pay rather dearly for it.

But the issue which cuts the deepest is a personal one, and that is the assumption so often made by fellow anglers who assume that to support field sports is to subscribe to the same politics. Listen, all I share is an addiction to the same sport – no more. I grew up in the sixties, went to university in the seventies and, pre-dictably enough, I am the real limp-wristed, pinko liberal deal. George Bush would probably characterise me as a pantywaist fag. I belong to the school of politics which holds that as long as they do not frighten the horses, then most things are OK. With some exceptions – capital punishment and racism are prominent among them. And so I do not believe that Tony Martin was a folk hero victim, I do not have a problem with the domes of Islam comple-menting the steepled cityscape, and I do not believe that the pound is a sacred jewel, nor that Europe is the Great Satan. I could go on, but you can guess the rest – I read the *Independent*, frown over Iraq (but don't have any better ideas of my own), worry about global warming (but not so much as to sell my mid-life-crisis sports car) and overcompensate so much to show my *bona fides* when I do meet a member of an ethnic minority that I am probably guilty of a different type of racism. In short, my feet are as well embedded in the clay as everyone else's.

There is a but, of course, and it is this. I would not dare to assume that fellow anglers are likely to share my politics any more than they are likely to have a shared passion for Joni Mitchell, Grand Prix motor racing, Martin Amis or *Coronation Street*. And so I am mystified why some of my fellow anglers so blithely assume that they can share their right-wing views with me without fear of contradiction – presumably in the belief that I subscribe to the same viewpoint, or perhaps they just know that we liberals have the heavy cross to bear of being programmed to defend the right to spout this crap in the first place.

The farcical debate about the fox-hunting ban seemed to me only to succeed in polarising opinions. Each side stereotyped both themselves and their opposition; they painted themselves into tight little corners of paranoia and self-righteousness. Hunt supporters characterised themselves as true country people, sons and daughters of the soil, knowledgeable about the mysterious ways of flora and fauna, and champions of rural post offices. Really? I have encountered just as many yawning chasms of ignorance about wildlife from field sportsmen as from the most blinkered inner city dweller.

And hunting itself . . . I have cantered across those frosty fields with the Badsworth and, as mentioned in an earlier chapter, I spent most of my childhood surrounded by the glare of pink coats and the reek of sweaty horse. People who hunt do not do so out of duty nor *noblesse oblige*, they do it for the same reason other people take drugs, downhill ski or race cars – because it's fun, and it's fun because it's dangerous, edgy. Hunting is a good reason to ride your horse flat out over the countryside, missing no opportunity to show off to your friends just how high your new horse can jump.

And the opposition? 'Ignorant townies', the hunters bellowed, as if residence were always a bar to understanding. Not necessarily ignorant, but often guilty of characterising those who hunted as bloodthirsty toffs, conveniently ignoring the fact that 10 miles' travel along any rural road will expose one to the sight of far more road-kill carnage than several seasons' worth of hunting. And the toff charge? Foxhunters are often suspiciously quick to refer to the Welsh Miners' Hunt and to the host of hunt supporters who live in council houses as examples of the sport's inclusiveness. Is it some sort of sin to be a toff – whatever that may mean in twenty-first-century Britain? Will the antis be targeting the ski runs of Klosters next or picketing gentlemen's clubs in Mayfair?

Let me end this ramble with an anecdote which, if it illustrates anything, shows only the fact that the issues are not straightforward. My wife is neither a hunter nor shooter nor fisher. She has accompanied me on the latter two activities, but her natural habitat is more Covent Garden than point-to-point or grouse moor. But she understands and respects my sport and has spent time with me by field or stream. She is a lapsed vegetarian but is selective in what she buys by reference to means of production, food miles and welfare. (God, that makes her sound worthy – she isn't, trust me.)

Last year she spent some time with a friend in Brighton (Hove, actually, I am reminded – a touchy point I believe). A well-known seaside resort, noted for the diversity of its population and the wealth of its cultural attractions. She was walking back from the theatre with her friend one day – it was still daylight and, as ever, the seagulls were playing fast and loose with the passing traffic. One of them pushed the envelope a little too far and lost the unequal battle with a passing car. It was not killed – it lay in the road badly injured and waving its one unbroken wing in a doomed attempt to escape. The streets were full – people tut-tutted and walked on. Drivers swerved round the doomed bird – although on what ground it is difficult to fathom. Did they want to prolong its agony? Joanne learned how to despatch a pheasant years ago, so, holding an imperious hand up to the traffic, she walked over to the bird, picked it up and wrung its neck. If she had not, how long would the bird have stayed there? Would any of the passing population – who, it is reasonable to assume, included some animal lovers amongst its number – have done a thing? As our local vicar would say: food for thought. Which is the sort of thing that vicars do say, of course, but few of them hunt, shoot, fish and drive a Morgan, unlike my local vicar, the splendidly named Reverend Toddy Hoare.

CHAPTER ELEVEN

COUNTER STRATEGY

*In all labour there is profit, but the talk
of the lips tendeth only to penury*

PROVERBS 14:23

'KILL YOUR DARLINGS' IS a piece of advice which has been
given to writers. Its provenance is unclear, as my Googling
suggests that a host of heavyweights may have said it first, ranging
from Mark Twain to William Faulkner to F. Scott Fitzgerald.
Because his name is – admit it – unimprovable I have decided that
Sir Arthur Quiller Couch was responsible for the phrase – which
means that the writer should cut to the chase, get to the point and,
critically, get rid of the passages that he is starting to feel just a little
smug about. And I experienced a variation of this myself: I could
not stop fiddling with this book because the text itself was veering
dangerously close to darling status. So, in what passes for real time
at Maison Aston, I am writing this chapter out of sequence, belat-
edly, because the darling book survived the kicking I had adminis-
tered after my last, definitive, never-to-be-repeated edit. So the

darling is more resilient than expected, but she is not going to survive this almost-too-late-for-the-ball chapter. Which is about . . . what? I guess it is about the fact that if I want to talk fishing I am better off staying at home, Laphroaig to hand (as it is now, actually) and Googling in to some fishing forum. Which will be studded with acronyms, sullied by emoticons and ablaze with flamings. I will recount the last flaming I read before returning to the theme which, bear with me, you will have to wait a little longer to discern fully.

A man had caught some chub on fly from a small stream; he had posted a picture of a good-looking fish of 2–3lbs on an internet forum. It lay inert on his net on the edge of the stream and it looked about as comfortable as a fish out of water ever can do. But the internet flaming roared and crackled like a Yule log is supposed to. Because? The angler had committed the apparently unforgivable sin of having failed to use an unhooking mat . . . on the near vertical bank of a steep-sided and overgrown brook. The reek of moralising self-righteousness shot through every critical post. There is only one acronym which is appropriate – and it is FFS (which, lest I be accused of coyness, stands for For Fuck's Sake). Do I need to explain? Probably not; if you have read this far either you are on a frequency somewhere adjacent to my broad wavelength or you are opening and closing your mouth in increasing bewilderment, and therefore beyond help.

Until the early 1990s, if I wanted to talk about fishing, learn about Daiwa's new wonder reel or Conoflex's new carp blank, hear about who caught what last weekend, be told about Big Dave's skirmish with a monster eel (thick as your arm, strong as an ox, no cliché spared), then all I had to do was to wander into my local tackle shop. The entry price was small; while it was rather bad form not to buy anything at all during my two-hour stay, a packet of Au Lion D'Or hooks and a couple of Arlesey bombs was enough to gain temporary membership. My first experiences were rather more humbling, though; in fact they were mortifying.

By the time I was eight or nine I was still fishless, in any meaningful way, but I had absorbed enough from the men who fished
t'Pastor (see Chapter One for translation) to realise that 6-inch
lobworms were not going to catch too many 5-inch roach. What
I needed were maggots, or 'maggits' as a West Riding tongue
would have had it. My father drove me to Castleford, to the hardware shop just over the bridge, which also sold fishing tackle.
Nervous, yes; but I was prepared, with half a crown clutched in
left hand and jam jar in the right. The proprietor, however, was
not prepared for my request for '4 ounces of maggots'. There was
a silence, seconds in duration but feeling rather closer to eternity.
His eyes closed briefly, a deep breath was taken and then came the
words which exposed me as the amateur, the ingénue, which I so
obviously was. 'We sell 'em by t'pint, lad'. He didn't smile, but I
bet he did in the Ship Inn over the road that night, Tetley's Mild
going down nicely and a Capstan drawing just so.

I learned quickly that shops which sold fishing tackle as a sideline
were to be avoided. It was just another piece of retail, just a profit
line between 16 June and a time shortly after the clocks went back
and the anglers gave up for the winter. There was no value added,
in the form of knowledge volunteered or anecdote retold. Mr
Schofield's shop on Wesley Street, however, did not treat fishing
peripherally but as the main act. I had found it whilst on a shopping
trip for my mother, and I literally stopped in my tracks as I saw the
irresistible display of Intrepid reels and Milbro match rods. And the
proprietor looked like the sort of yeoman figure who is now used to
portray a jolly butcher or baker in one of those Never Neverland,
Sunday-night, feel-good dramas on TV. Even the smell of the shop
was different – there was that slight nose-wrinkling stab of maggots
from the back room underlined with a warm organic wash of breadcrumb ground bait and Woodbine smoke.

I wore my ignorance like a flag but Mr Schofield did not pat-
ronise me; he managed to make me feel as though I were part of

the brotherhood, despite the fact that I then had a posh accent and knew less than bugger all about fishing. I became a regular visitor, of course, and loved my Saturday morning visits, when the shop would be full of flat-capped miners picking up their orders of maggots for the big match at Dunsforth or Hammerton the following day. And I still have two items from that shop, both bought for me by my mother, one for Christmas 1967 and the other for birthday 1968. The first item is a Fibatube fly rod, 9 feet long and with an action the sloppy side of soft; the other is the definitive centrepin reel – the Allcocks Match Aerial. It has a form defined only by function but with a detailed finesse that only an artist could conjure. It has the perfection of scale and style you find on a Bugatti Type 35, an iPod or Concorde, a machine so perfect that it claims the definite article as of right.

In university days my local tackle shop was Kendall and Watson, located in one of the arcades in Leeds City Centre. And my £10 says that you cannot buy Chrysodine maggots or brandling worms in that arcade now, although if you have a pressing need for a Lulu Guinness handbag or a Hermès belt, your search might just be over.

Leeds had a thriving angling community in the 1970s, centred upon the Leeds and District Amalgamated Society of Anglers for entertainment and match bookings, and Kendall and Watson for bait and tackle. The latter was primarily a match fishing shop, but it also catered for the growing community of self-appointed specimen hunters. Although it was not too far from where I was brought up, Leeds had a pace that was faster and much more urgent. Even the speech patterns had a jabbing, insistent dogmatism and a volume which suggested violence was but a spilled pint away. It never was, of course; it was just the legacy of requiring most of the male workforce to sweat its long weeks out in the clangs and throbs of heavy engineering factories, mines and mills. So Kendall and Watson's shop could sound like a street fight on weekends as orders were shouted and instructions bellowed by a shop full of psyched up matchmen. But visit the same place in my student slacker mode on a Wednesday afternoon, and I would learn so much. About where was fishing well, and which peg number in the desolate miles of riverbank between Dunsforth and Aldwark had produced the big bream haul or the 5lb chub.

Volumes were quieter in Lincoln but the intensity was greater. Harrison's shop was the epicentre of the Lincolnshire specimen scene in the mid-seventies, and it was tucked away in an area which is on the border between industrial and residential. Harrisons offered a bilateral approach to its customers – after entering the shop the casual visitor would be presented with a counter and display area full of the sort of gear you needed to catch bream from the Lower Witham or roach from one of the local pits: matchrods, the odd pole and the inevitable Mitchell Match and ABU closed-face reels. But walk past the counter into the back of the shop, and you would enter a sanctum presided over by a man called Pat. He lived in the remains of a Second-World-War airfield a few miles west of Lincoln, kept some chickens, shot some pigeon and caught a lot of fish. He was softly spoken, with the quiet, lilting vowels of Lincolnshire – such a contrast to the sharp-edged aggression of the West Riding. The walls were covered in photos – big carp from nameless or pseudonymous pits, enormous pike from drains such as Timberland Delph, and olive-gold tench spirited out of estate lakes on the edge of the Wolds on hot June mornings. Stick around long enough in Pat's shop and you would meet all the scions of the Lincolnshire scene and bathe in the glorious fact that you weren't just reading about the speci-men scene in *Angling* and *Coarse Fisherman* any more, you were part of it. Other than actually catching the fish, of course, but assuming the persona was surely the vital step towards doing so?

But one thing Harrison's did not do well was maggots; they were a bait deeply out of fashion with the specimen-hunting clique

– because, I suspect, we were still too focused on the big-baits-for-big-fish philosophy of Walker and Stone. And whilst particle baits such as sweetcorn and black-eyed beans were on the radar, they were talked about in whispers. Maggots were for the noddies – as all pleasure and match anglers were loftily termed. But, as I had a secret life as a noddy, a private vice of catching roach and rudd from a favourite gravel pit on light float tackle, I really needed some top-quality maggots. I had heard the rumours about a producer of maggots of an almost supernatural quality since my arrival in Lincoln, and I knew that their creator was based somewhere in the west of the City. More enquiries – friends of friends, acquaintances of men in pubs – revealed the alchemist's location, a lock-up garage near the County Offices where I then worked.

I called in one lunchtime, knocked on the weathered dark timber door and met Mr Domin. He was Polish and specialised in bicycle repair work and maggot husbandry. He showed me zinc baths full of maggots of a quality I had never witnessed before; the usual ammonia-tinged smell was almost entirely absent, and if maggots could look happy these ones were near ecstatic. There were choices – mighty gozzers, creamy white and engorged and tiny industrious pinkies writhing in their thousands. I opted for the gozzers, paid – rather a lot – and I caught a wonderful bag of roach from the tiny pit in the grounds of the Malleable Castings factory. (In a bizarre inversion, Poles are now ubiquitous but men selling maggots as a sideline from a lock-up are, I suspect, completely extinct.)

Trevor Moss was a fellow member of the Witham Valley Specimen Group and started his business in Gainsborough in the late seventies. I don't think Trevor spent too much time on consumer research or focus group discussion before electing to call his business The Tackle Shop but it quickly became an important part of the specimen scene, both regionally and nationally. This fact alone reflected that the whole polarity of angling was changing;

if more fishermen had been sociologists at the time there would have been earnest chin-stroking and discussion of the imminence of a paradigm shift; I believe they speak of little else in Gainsborough.

In the sixties, Mr Schofield's customers had fished within a narrow radius of home during the week – a short bike ride or a long walk often being the only option – whilst at weekends the radius would expand to take in the Trent and the Yorkshire Ouse for the fur 'n' feather match. They would pile in to some groaning single-decker bus, holdalls and baskets over shoulders, and they would play as closely together as they worked. So sixties angling was a parochial activity, apart from a week's holiday on the Norfolk Broads or up at Loch Ken for the bream. But by the mid-seventies most anglers owned a car, or had a mate who did, and the serious fishermen would travel as far as was necessary to find the best waters or to buy the new pair of fast-taper carp rods which they did not so much need as crave like the addicts they had become.

Trevor's shop was as likely to be visited by some ducking and diving geezers from Essex, on a foray Up North for the state-of-the-art bite detectors as it was to be frequented by the local lad asking for some 18s to nylon. And the local specimen hunters were more likely to be telling tall tales of their adventures with Tring roach at Startops Reservoir, or about tussling with the big mirrors at Waveney Valley Lakes or drifting Loch Lomond, as they were to be discussing the prospects on Witham or Trent. It was a good time to be a serious angler, as we idiotically would have termed ourselves – and I now pride myself on being a very frivolous one. Anything seemed possible, so quickly were the horizons of the sport being expanded; people were starting to talk about the untapped potential of Europe, and stories started to be whispered about the giant carp being caught from Lac Cassien in the south of France. And so there was a buzz to The Tackle Shop, the sound of dreams being planned, of ambitions being realised and reputations being staked out. I missed it when I moved north and would often justify the 160-mile round trip on the grounds that I really did need those new rigbins, a better rucksack or those funky, brutally functional rod rests.

Because, Match Aerial aside, whilst the gear we had used until then was, in Sale of Goods Act terms, both fit for purpose and of merchantable quality, it had a utilitarian functionality that felt so at odds with a sport whose purpose was only pleasure. The more discerning anglers had already started to upgrade to ABU 55 fixed-spool reels, preferring the cool precision of Swedish engineering to the small-saver economy of the Mitchell 300. But we were consumers, and were soon drawn like July thunderbugs to the bright colours and sheer funkiness of more contemporary designs. Whilst multiplier reels always seemed to me to be the answer to a question nobody had asked, I coveted the glitzy style of a Daiwa Millionaire like a *Hello* magazine reader covets her Manolo Blahniks or Jimmy Choos. We wanted added value, we craved the features which 'surprise and delight', as Giles in Marketing would have put it.

When I moved to North Yorkshire I needed a local dealer, and I didn't have to wait too long for The Man. He was Derek Stratton and he ran a shop in Thirsk – until forced into retirement by a declining customer base and the fact that most of his remaining customers had migrated to the local carp-filled hole in the ground, where it was possible not only to catch tame carp but also to buy the bait to do so. Derek's shop, in its heyday, was rare in that it served all anglers, from Whitby-bound cod fishermen in search of chrome-plated pirks, to the local worthies wheezing up to the Spey and Tweed to catch their annual salmon. Derek was, and is, a lovely man but he holds strong political views, often diametrically opposed to my own, and it remains the only shop I have visited where I would receive a refresher course in Thatcherism, the decline in education or the follies of the Environment Agency.

In a variation on the buy-one-get-one-free offer, you could buy a spool of Maxima and get a free polemic. Derek's shop is a tattoo parlour now. Or is it massage? Or perhaps both? Have they supplanted the sport which reputedly once had two million participants? Will any flesh remain undecorated, any muscle not tautened by soothing hands?

This chapter is loosely about the act of buying tackle and the fact that its purchase was usually just a visa to enjoy the company of other anglers. We didn't call it networking then: a term which would have had a pleasing symmetry – but that's what it was, and it isn't anymore. When I learnt that this book had attracted a publisher, wasn't going to remain some photocopied sheets in a dusty lever arch file to be discarded by my executors, I decided to celebrate. Champagne made me realise that I wanted, in fact quite urgently needed, yet another fly rod. I already owned eleven, but that was of no consequence, as there was a critical gap in the armoury. I owned a 7ft 6in Hardy Sovereign, and an 8ft 6in Hardy Deluxe, but – how could I have survived so far? – nothing of 8ft, let alone a Hardy. And so I drove over the Pennines on a snowy Sunday in January to remedy the omission by visiting a firm whose corporate blushes I will spare but whose name is above the bigger advertisements in the game-fishing press.

The place is easy enough to find, you just follow the almost new Range Rovers and BMW X5s, park where they do and follow the braying drivers to the shop. Funny crew, some of these guys; their natural habitat is the Game Fair, or perhaps the more expensive shoots in the Shires. Plus-fours, if not actually *de rigueur*, are common and, if worn, are highlighted by the long socks with those curious adornments of brightly coloured garter flashes. Do they wear these for a bet? Or to recognise each other when surrounded by the masses, chased by chavs or harried by hodges?

The retail experience was as bleak as it was efficient. Having managed to interrupt the bored reverie of an assistant, I explained that I was looking for a Hardy eight-footer, that I wanted an action more 'through' than 'tip' and that, actually, price was not the key criterion. Not a flicker of interest. In unemotional, flat tones, I was told that all the Hardy rods they had in stock were already on display and that I should pick the one that I liked the best. I had Googled some reviews, so choosing the rod was not difficult, but it was utterly joyless and I was back on the road again within fifteen minutes of arrival. The rod will be fine, I know, but if this is the future of fishing shops then I will order online next time . . . before looking for someone I can flame on a forum.

CHAPTER TWELVE

FLYING LESSONS

Ah, la belle chose que de savoir quelque chose

MOLIÈRE, *Le Bourgeois Gentilhomme*

I BECAME AWARE OF fly fishing in the same haphazard fashion as I learnt about the facts of life. Not the homily from foot-shuffling parents, consumed by embarrassment, not the crisp précis delivered by my tight-skirted biology teacher (who, unaccountably, seemed to occupy my mind for surprisingly long intervals on the bus trip to school), but by a gradual process of osmosis. You start to hear the stories, discount them (surely not the Queen?), you dismiss them as fabrications of your friends, you see the odd picture, you read the odd book and suddenly you are aware that you know about this stuff. In a theoretical fashion only, of course. The practical bit takes much longer – far too long in my case.

Despite the democratisation of fly fishing which Grafham, Chew and the rest had sparked, it was still a tactic which registered as only the tiniest blip on my consciousness in the early 1970s. Angling Soc did own a couple of fly rods, and what ghastly things they were; no elegant cane, and carbon fibre was still little more than a dream in Richard Walker's mind. The rods were ratty little glass fibre outfits with clumsy metal ferrules. Think of them as eight-year-old Daewoo cars, and you will get the idea: they were not cutting-edge. And the fly lines complemented their mediocrity; tight-coiled and cracked, their use was confined to a couple of trips in the coarse close season to the River Rye at Nunnington or the Nidd at Pateley Bridge. Inevitably, it was my friend, the patrician Jon, who was responsible for persuading me to try this strange technique on a cold April day. He patiently explained the basics, the crisp movements punctuated by critical pauses, the role of the left hand and the discipline of the right wrist. Far too much for me fully to comprehend, so I gave the usual novice performance, concentrating on aerialising the line by frantic, pause-free whipping. The back cast would involve the rod pointing horizontally behind me, and only rarely did the fly spend any time in the water. This is the hardest thing about fly fishing – unlike most other techniques, you are not even fishing in any meaningful way until you have spent too many hours – and they feel like wasted ones – trying to educate your right arm and left hand. There is simply no mental space left even to consider where the fly should be cast nor how, or even if, it should be retrieved.

Jon was a smart man, a charming one too, and he was deter-mined to teach me how to master the fly, as even in that early stage of our friendship there was a tacit understanding that we would be lifelong friends and it was therefore important for him to share his enthusiasm, but also to make fly fishing a communal bond. As it did; and as it has for all of my closest fishing friends.

Although my early fly-fishing experiences had intrigued more than captivated, Jon maintained the pressure to learn, and in the middle 1970s he invited me to his parents' home in Surrey as a base from which to fish the small still waters which were starting to be developed in the south. Jon's parents were formidable – father,

Mike, was a Brigadier; mother, Virginia, piercingly, intimidatingly bright and with a blue-chip family background. She is one of the few people I have met who can pepper her conversation with words like paradigm, axiomatic or epistemological without sounding even remotely pretentious. The Stevens lived in a stunning house, surrounded by dense woodland: the sort of property one sees in *Country Life* in fact (note, by the way, how the 'one' crept in so insidiously there). Hydon Barn even had a bloody granary. I had expected, mistakenly, that Surrey was entirely comprised of Terry-and-June suburbia and I simply was not prepared for this heavily wooded haven. But I loved it. Conversation at dinner was in stark contrast to our usual topics at home of surgery times and hunting dates; it was much more exotic – people seemed interested in my views on *Macbeth*, nuclear disarmament or Samuel Beckett. Fuelled by pre-prandial gin, followed by claret – from a real wine cellar – I would mumble some adolescent inanities based upon what I could remember from the sixth form before being rescued by some startlingly original *aperçu* from Virginia, which would leave me reeling. But it was hugely flattering to be treated as a house guest whose views were important enough to be sought, even if it were out of politeness or charm. Jon's sister was at RADA then, and I remember Marlboro-and-red-wine-fuelled discussions into the early hours on whatever our current Big Issues were. I had to lie about these, as my own big issue was realising that drinking late-night wine with Juliet seemed to have the edge on chasing any trout.

The fishing, therefore, was not the sole appeal, but my first sight of Damerham was still a revelation. Never had I seen water clearer, never had I seen bigger trout, and never had I felt so completely out of my piscatorial depth. Colin Harms, the then owner of the chain of lakes, blithely talked about how well the water had been fishing, with fish of 5lbs and more being caught regularly. These might sound small fish by twenty-first century standards but in the seventies a 2lb trout was not a fish to be ignored.

As we walked down to the first lake I was enchanted, but a feeling of unreality enveloped me. It was not that I felt I did not belong there – I was a fisherman and I could catch fish, if not always on the chosen method – but there was a sense that this was all some construct: that water was never meant to be so clear, weed never meant to be so startlingly green. It felt like walking beside landscaped swimming pools, and, although I came to adore Damerham, the sense of artificiality never quite left me. Nor has it when confronted even with natural waters of similar translucence and luxuriance; I adore Cape Wrath's Loch Borralaidh, and I have loved the odd chalk stream I have fished, but they never seemed quite to have the solidity, the weight of *being* that cloudier, murkier waters, so easily evoke. Fishing clear water can feel like fishing in air; too much is visible, not enough remains a mystery. Except on Borralaidh, of course, in the places where the pellucid shallows plunge into invisible blue dark depths.

Back to Damerham. Jon pointed out Bill Sibbons to me, then a near-legendary fisherman on the chalky still waters of the south. Bill stood hunched like a heron and stared into the water for long silent hours until a killer cast would flick out and another rainbow was deceived – usually the biggest in the shoal. I was happy to start this stillwater adventure on a less selective basis, and I was instructed to fish a Baby Doll. Jon recycled the usual nonsense which the correspondence columns of *Trout and Salmon* perpetrated back then, to the effect that fish mistook this fluorescent white blob for a hatching sedge pupa. I had never seen one at the time, but I still had my doubts. And I was right, of course, as I came to learn that rainbow trout take such a fly because . . . well, it's there, and it might taste good. Or it might be fun to bite or chase. They are not the brightest of fish, but who needs to die old when you can live so fast?

It was utterly absorbing fishing. I learned quickly that one stops thinking about casting when a 20-inch rainbow is cruising along the rushy margins, looking confident, curious and hungry. Time and again I spooked fish, but at least some of them locked on to the fly, followed it, eyed it up before realising their hunter was an amateur and arrowed back to the middle of the lake. Strange how disdainful a farm-bred trout can appear. But we were in Hampshire, and I was from the North. Perhaps it showed?

I blanked on my first trip. Jon did not, but he allowed, expansively, that it had been difficult fishing on that hot, clear-skied day.

My practical introduction to day-to-day fly fishing was at Toft Newton in Lincolnshire or further south on Grafham Water. One a concrete bowl, the other a near legend. I fished with a small group of friends from Lincoln who were as fired up as I was by the tidal wave of enthusiasm for reservoir fly fishing which was surging through the angling monthlies. In that period of hothouse learning, shared experiences and commitment, there was an imperative to do things better, to catch more fish, to cast further. The longer the leader we could manage, and the more furiously we could double haul, the more credibility we gained. We were all coarse fishermen, but we would not admit we fished just for pleasure – we were specimen hunters and we had a deadly serious approach to our sport. Not always a good thing, but it served us well on our steep learning curve. We quickly realised that fly fishing is one branch of the sport where, most of the time, the numbers far outweigh the scales. Our early techniques were all variations on simple lure-stripping. We fished sinking lines with short leaders and we used the standard lure patterns of the day – Black Chenilles, Whisky flies, Leprechauns, Muddlers and inevitably the Baby Doll. We caught, too; usually small, stumpy-finned fish with a tendency to turn black on despatch. But it was immensely absorbing fishing; unlike our leisurely, bedchaired languor whilst carp or pike fishing, here we had to be busy. We had to stand up, cast, retrieve, tie leaders (frequently), walk, wade and occasionally even play fish. Killing the fish was a new task too. Even in those days most coarse fish were treated with the utmost delicacy and respect. To kill a coarse fish, other than for bait, was treasonable. It seemed strange at the time, but not with hindsight, that we were able so easily to adapt to the world of catch and kill. There was something irresistibly attractive about the heavy weight of a fish bass full of trout which you – yes, you – had caught on fly.

We realised quickly that we were indulging in the obvious. We had read that, actually, the smart trout fishermen did not do this mindless lure-stripping – they nymph fished. This involved another enormous leap of faith. Once the bare technique of casting was mastered, lure fishing did not really represent a huge departure from spinning for pike or perch. It was better, of course, because of the greater intimacy involved; a take to a Mepps usually involved a telegraphed series of taps to the rod tip, or sometimes just the sudden arresting of a retrieve, rod bouncing into unanticipated weight. But fly fishing felt, *was* different. Each take was experienced by the right forefinger – the one which is programmed to explore anything and everything for touch and feel. And so the hard rapping of an angry rainbow engulfing a Whisky fly was immediate, and could be startling in its intimacy. But, sensuality aside, lure fishing became an easy task. And because it was easy, we started to lose concentration, we lost respect for the method; it was clearly for the masses, and we wanted to be fisherman who excelled, we wanted to belong to an elite. We did try deviating into ultra-fast-sink lines, stripped Muddlers across the surface and tandem lures, but they all did so little to stave off what felt like staleness.

We had seen people fishing with floating lines. They usually were ten years older than us, studious and obviously concentrating hard; the mystery was, upon what? They caught fish, enough to attract our curiosity, but we could not understand what was being done, so little activity did there seem to be. We read Arthur Cove and Geoff Bucknall, and started to glean the theory. We looked at insects in a new light – were those things Buzzers? Just what, exactly, did a Sedge Pupa look like? And, most importantly, just how do you know when a fish takes a fly which is not being stripped back?

We found out at a small still water near Doncaster called Lindholme. It was a satisfying venue to fish after the two-dimensional void of Toft Newton's concrete bowl, because it had rushes, banks with features and a wealth of birdsong, in contrast to the twittering monotony of the Toft Newton skylarks. It felt a good place to try nymph fishing. I had already bought a light rod – a Geoffrey Bucknall Two Lakes in Heron Grey, and a No. 7 line, which seemed gossamer thin compared to the eights and nines I had convinced myself I really needed. Fish were head-and-tailing – so *that* is what it meant – within easy casting range. I could not see the Buzzers, but I had already read enough to convince myself that I was watching a hatch being harvested by trout. I started to spot individual fish working, their progress clearly punctuated every few feet by the alluring sight of dorsal fin spearing through the surface. I tied on a Size 14 black Buzzer and cast. I retrieved, automatically, and cursed myself. Autopilot disengaged, fully in control, I recast and I saw the tiny punctuation mark entry of the fly into the surface film. I had greased the leader and it floated neatly along the smooth ripple. A fish appeared, 2 feet from where the fly had landed. I drew 6 inches of line, slowly, with my left hand. And then, entrancingly, the leader slid over the surface; it was unmistakably, unmissably, a take. I was right only about the unmistakeability, for I struck into no resistance, seeing the fish swirl in alarm. This was subtle, this was difficult, this could become addictive; I had been given the source code of a secret and I was not going to lose it.

Expertise building by the trip, I returned to Damerham in that strange hot August of 1976. Although it was late summer, the odd disorientated mayfly still fluttered from the water, and damsel flies darted intensely from reed to reed. I took my cue from them and I fished a nondescript green nymph on a long-shanked Size 10 hook. I fished slowly, subtly, and I learned to concentrate on the areas less fished. Tight corners, curtained by trees, or bounded by thick weed beds. The denser the setting, the more confident the fish seemed to be, and I had a good enough day, unprecedentedly, to have had to have bought a second ticket. It was such a smug feeling, and the reek and weight of my fish bass felt like a campaign medal. And at last I could utter those heavily loaded words 'Double Limit'. Later, Jon took me to Two Lakes, where slow-burning disbelief replaced smugness. It was a retired gentlefolks' outdoor dining club. There was a scattering of deckchairs, punctuated by bottles of Gordons gin and the merest hint of a suggestion that, although making the odd cast was expected, if not actually compulsory, trying to catch one's limit was really rather bad form. And I did try so very hard to avoid catching mine, but the fish came to the fly with the witless trust of puppies wanting to be stroked. Two Lakes was a very strange place indeed; a good tick on one's fishing CV, but somewhere where normality seemed to have been put permanently on hold.

CHAPTER THIRTEEN

RIVER TRANCE

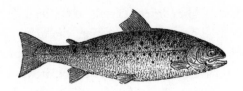

I do not know much about Gods but I think
that the river is a strong brown God

T. S. Eliot, 'Dry Salvages'

WHEN I RETURNED TO Yorkshire in 1979 I lived within a short walk of the Swale, and, although I had imagined that I would spend my time doing the same old chub and barbel routine, I had little appetite for either. Actually, it was not the fish themselves, it was the style of fishing. Whilst I am happy enough to sit and watch a quivertip, float or bobbin in the winter, static sport simply does not appeal in the summer time.

My working life was and is sedentary, and I need physical exercise to drive away the angst of meetings and the tedium of reviewing fifty-page documents full of leaden terms like escrow, dispute resolution, benchmarking and performance indicators. The law never was a vocation, and I would be embarrassed to admit if it had been. We baby boomers want it all. We want – need – immortality; we crave – have a right to – endless self-gratification. It can leave an unpleasant taste after a few decades but, hey, I escaped the war, I avoided National Service, the bomb didn't drop, the climate has not yet changed completely, and I have a full tank of petrol. Worrying, isn't it, when you apply my Olympian selfishness to millions of people like me?

The Swale . . . yes. Apart from my tyro's flailing of the Rye in university days, I had not fished rivers at all in my fly-fishing career, and the one thing I knew about North Yorkshire was that it was too long a drive to Toft Newton or Grafham. I was aware that people did fly fish rivers, of course, but most of my reading had been confined to the predictable accounts of the southern chalk streams. And so I knew my Plunket Greene, Grey of Fallodon, Sawyer and Skues, but I knew nearly nothing about fishing a spate river with a fly.

When I tried it, early in 1980, with entirely unsuitable tackle, I was staggered at the sheer amount of activity involved. Not only was the casting much more frequent, but it had to be more accurate, the line had to be mended to avoid drag, and the rod tip held higher than the 8 o'clock slouch which characterised my stillwater fishing. And I was busy because I was catching fish – and lots of them. Despite using flies which were totally unsuitable – too big, wrong patterns – in each session I would catch up to a dozen fish, sometimes twenty or even more. The occasional one was a trout, but most were grayling, small chub and dace. And here was another unexpected aspect of fly fishing; I had always equated it to trout fishing only, but in reality it has turned out to be one of the most adaptable methods of all. To date, I have caught the following fish on fly – brown trout, rainbow trout, brook trout, grayling, chub, dace, roach, perch, pike, bleak, tench, carp, barbel, bream, sea trout and salmon. Some were singletons – such as the near-double-figure mirror carp from Farmire, which gave a virtuoso impression of a big brown trout until it emerged from the depths like a scaly piglet. And one – the barbel – was, I admit, hooked fairly in the left pectoral fin. I can still remember the fight though.

So little relevant, or so it seemed to me, had been written about fly fishing northern rivers, that I improvised, I trialled and only too often I erred. Of course there *were* books on this type of fishing, but they were all . . . well, sort of old. And as a specimen hunter who expected, even demanded, new developments to appear in each monthly copy of *Angling*, I could not admit the possibility that old could still be good.

I read the old stuff because I enjoyed its time-lapsed charm and the quality of the prose but I did not realise that north-country tactics had evolved decades ago and had not changed much since. Like sharks, they had already reached a perfect stage of evolution. But, writing in 2007, I now have a whole armoury of innovation to exploit; I am not sure why river fishing became sexy and dynamic, but I espoused Goldheads, Klinkhamers and Czech Nymphs with interest (the last) and total devotion (the penultimate). Goldheads are . . . well . . . so nineties don't you think? Do they await the same fate as the Whisky fly and the Baby Doll, rusting in old fly wallets? The Snipe and Purple will outlive them all.

My original river tactic was, predictably, wet fly, fished down and across. First with one fly, a Black Pennell or an Invicta perhaps, and then with one, sometimes even two droppers. In a long-defunct tackle shop in Thirsk I had also bought some local spider patterns: the inevitable Snipe and Purple, Partridge and Orange, and their many cousins. Although they looked wisps of inconsequentiality, so did what they were supposed to represent. After the in-your-face colour of Dunkelds, they looked a little muted, self-effacing even – but since when did olive nymphs start a fight in a pub or moon out of minibuses? And, of course, in the water those delicate flies did not literally represent the real thing – such representation is too static, too wooden – they created impressions, caricatures which, like the best cartoons, create instant recognition in the spectator. Just think of Gerald Scarfe, Robert Crumb or *The Simpsons*. Get it? The trout and grayling did.

I fished down and across because I could not translate chalkstream dogma into a language that I could speak on the Ure or the

Near Rievaulx, the green paradise
that is the River Rye in springtime.
(*Neil Perry*)

The dignified way to present one's catch. Above, the author with a 3lb wild brown trout from Loch Caladail, Cape Wrath and, below, a 14lb mirror carp taken on floating crust.

Dignity was less easy to preserve when grappling with
a 28lb 10oz pike from the River Ure.

Sionascaig – the perfect name for the perfect loch.

The sun sets behind Quinag on a calm evening on wild Loch Assynt.

Final preparations for the first drift on Sionascaig.

Looking north from the west bank of Loch Borralaidh.

Loch Keisgaig – not quite the middle of nowhere but close.

Changing my fly on the upper Cod Beck in Mayfly time.
(*Neil Perry*)

The late Jon Stevens fishing a more open stretch of Cod Beck.

Playing and landing a 1lb 6oz wild brown trout on Cod Beck.
(*Neil Perry*)

Swale. I could not even see the bloody fish, let alone the tell-tale white of a trout's opening jaw as Frank Sawyer claimed to do. When I first visited the Wiltshire Avon I began to understand that whole Sawyer, Oliver Kite theme, but it was not a tune you could play on a spate river. Think of a hundred yards of River Ure. Starting with an 8-foot-deep tumbling pot of water, hard-flowing over limestone boulders. It slows down, creates a back eddy here, a slack there. The water shallows again and runs 15 yards wide over stone and gravel, broken-surfaced and rippled, and then stalls into 30-yard-wide flats. There is current, but a glassy smooth surface which makes your leader look like a hawser; and the odd rise you do see is on the far bank under the trees.

You wade in and the ripples semaphore your arrival and purpose to everything apart from the ubiquitous tiny grayling. Even with polaroids, you are lucky to see the odd fish, and when you do, you see it from the bank between the branches of a willow tree. And so chalk-stream craft, good though it is on even-currented mown-banked parkland, is of little application Up North. Or so I thought, until I did learn to exploit some 'minor tactics', as Skues would have termed it, but that is for another chapter.

Down and across – three times I have typed those words – it is a repetitious game, and it covers a lot of water; it searches it in great diagonal swathes, and it is a lovely way to learn to fish a river. Because you have to concentrate, but not really so hard that you cannot admire the kingfisher flashing downstream, not so intently that you can't plan the rather fiddly main course for dinner tonight. And also, regrettably, not so much that you can always escape the toad work or whatever black dog angst is stalking you this year.

The takes are easy enough to discern. None of this spotting a subaqueous wink or watching for an inch of leader to sink just a little too quickly to be quite plausible. It is a much less subtle game. Tweaks, pulls and yanks according to current, species, size and amount of attention being paid by angler. If you are diligent, you can watch the fly line twitch upwards, a slack line swingtip. Or watch the swirl on the surface. Do so if you want, but you would catch almost as many fish if you just waited for the rod tip to bang round. This is because down and across is a paper tiger of a method. It attracts fish like little else, induces them to snatch at the fast disappearing fly. But . . . because it is hurried, because it is often curiosity or irritation rather than hunger which is responsible, the hooking rate is really quite dreadful. On a bad day you can hit one in six takes, or even fewer. And if you connect, especially in fast water, the fish will so often fall off. Because, not only is it downstream (and, if it is a grayling, it has the huge pressure of water on its immense dorsal), but your strike has also pulled the hook away from the fish's mouth, sometimes into it en route but often only by the most tenuous of hookholds.

Down and across – that's five times – you see, you can get bored with this technique, ask any salmon fisherman. (They don't like to admit it but it's all they are doing.) Down and across – stop it, *now* – also attracts little fish and spooks the big ones. So, if you want lots of action, not enough results, small fish and plenty of lost fish, almost invariably the bigger ones, the method which, after this mauling, no longer dare speak its name is the one you really should use. But it was a good technique to employ to learn a river, to understand the contours of the pools and, most importantly, to understand where fish actually live.

Think about those last words. I had to think about them, a lot, because the truth was I had not a clue where fish could live. I realised, slowly, that I was fishing with what I could rather archly term chub goggles. Rivers meant chub at this stage in my fishing career, and chub lived in 4 or 5 feet of water, usually towards the far bank and often under or adjacent to a willow or an alder. True, to a degree, especially in respect of chub which have just been scared by the angler hammering in rod rests after lurching over the skyline. Shallow water was just that – it did not contain fish because you never caught them there. Mainly because you didn't fish there, but even if you had, your Arlesey bomb and luncheon meat would have scared everything in the pool anyway (at least for a period longer than it took for your threshold of boredom to be reached, whereupon you would recast to the reassuring familiarity of the deep-water bush).

I started to realise that what I did know about rivers and the fish that lived in them was so superficial, so founded in false assumptions and generalisations as to be meaningless. As a coarse fisherman I wasted little time in speculating what chub or barbel ate between my visits to the river. So focused had I become on the efficacy of one bait over another that I had to remind myself that between their treats of luncheon meat, sausage or sweetcorn, the fish had a staple diet of whatever they could hunt or harvest from the river. In an unfocused and uninterested way, I knew they must eat bugs and insects, but what they were called, even what they looked like, was of no interest to me.

Only as a pike fisherman had I matched the hatch by fishing baits which were accepted as daily fare by the pike. But, as I thought about it, I realised that parallels could be drawn between pike fishing tactics and fly fishing for trout. There was the choice between exact replication – dead dace or well-tied daddy long legs, or the deceit of caricature – a Deeper Dan plug or a Silver Invicta.

In stillwater fly fishing, the purity of imitation had always appealed more than parody's hammed up performance, and I wanted to continue this philosophy on the rivers. But stillwater fly recognition had seemed so much easier, or so it seemed in my narrow perception, as it was principally confined to buzzers (big or small; green, brown or black) and sedge (dry or pupa). But river flies . . . all I knew was that I had an enormous amount to learn. I realised that the Snipe and Purple was meant to imitate small hatching nymphs, but of what? What did they look like, where were they found and how did they live? And, already a fisherman for two decades, why the hell did I apparently know so very little?

As a coarse fisherman I was rarely more than a passive spectator of what happened in a river. I could read the flow, spot those subtle little creases between slack and current where fish loved to congregate, but little more than that. I didn't see, wasn't even aware of, the daily dramas of subaqueous life. I was not participating in any meaningful way because I didn't need to. Provided my cheese paste and ground bait constituted an inducement to feast, a trap for the greedy, I needed to do little more than wait for the quivertip to stab in response to the next fish I had fooled. But fly fishing did not work like this, there was no groundbaiting, no sweet-smelling bait, only the odourless deceit of fur and feather. And that could only ever work if fly, time and location were in perfect alignment. This could be harder than work – but with the added seasoning of excitement, of discovery, of fulfilment.

I never waded into a river to fish until I started to fly fish; I did not even stand up to fish most of the time. Swims were selected, shamefully, by the criteria of comfort of bank, suitability of angle for chair and ease of location of rod rest. But I started to wade when I became a fly fisher, and immediately there was a profound change in my whole approach; I was aware of strength of current, temperature of water and topography of river-bed. There was an element of risk, too, as hard current pushed and pressured me, gravel slipped from under my feet, foothold was lost against unexpected boulder or root. But it felt like being on the stage itself, spotlit and focused, instead of hunched in the stalls, passive and inert, and because I was playing a role, was part of the plot, I didn't need to work too hard on following it.

And because I was now in the river I started to get the first inklings of what lived there. Like an eight-year-old, I would kneel in the shallows, turning rocks over and observing the whole community of life which made its home there. Like most people who grew up in the 1960s and 1970s, I had an awareness of ecology, or at least an imperative to admit its importance; I had read *Silent Spring*, knew what the subtext was to 'Big Yellow Taxi'. But by observing at first hand the interdependence of life, sometimes symbiotic, but more often founded on the relationship of predator and prey, it all started to make profound sense. I identified the struggling olive nymphs, inconsequential but important, I saw scudding little shrimps, and I delighted in the perfect architecture of the tubular shelters of stick and sand the caddis grubs had so painstakingly constructed. (But how else could they have spent their time? Were there choices?) Further up the river, I encountered the surreal sight of stonefly nymphs, impossibly large and looking like remnants from prehistory. Crayfish, too, huddled under the larger rocks in the calm corners under the willows, claws held up in challenge to the wading intruder.

Of course, the nymphs sheltered *here* because there was food, oxygen and safety; they hatched simultaneously, they bred and died. Trout would eat them at each stage; all I had to do was to work out which fly in which stage of its life was on today's menu and how to fish my artificial in a way which made it distinctive enough to be singled out, but not such a freak as to be repellent and unpalatable.

Before, I had seen flies as an inner-city kid might see birds; pigeon or peregrine, chaffinch or sparrow hawk, they are all just background, peripheral and unimportant. But now . . . now every difference was important, and the more I learnt the more I could apply, and the more I could become part of the river. I felt I could empathise with heron or osprey, because we were in the same business, the only difference being that they did it to survive and I did it to learn how to live. It's a sensual game, fly fishing, and I indulged every sense. Playing fish by hand, because it felt immediate, alive, and not desensitised by the mechanics of a fixed spool reel. Lifting the rod tip high against the power of a hooked fish, and trying to commit every sight, smell and feel to memory. Fishing had always seemed to me to be about sensation, but fishing fly in a river offered sensations outside any previous experience. Hooked? Permanently.

CHAPTER FOURTEEN

BEYOND THE LOOKING GLASS

*I don't pretend to understand the Universe – it's a great deal bigger
than I am.*

THOMAS CARLYLE

I OWN UP. I read *The Da Vinci Code* too; I was on holiday, and it
was all I could find, I plead in mitigation. Liar. But remember
how part of the Code was only decipherable by holding a mirror
up to it? I thought you might, and like me you held your copy up
to the bathroom mirror. Admit it. Fly fishing upstream on a river
you thought you knew can feel like a fourth-dimension experience
if you only learnt the river looking downstream. Physically it
cannot be different. Same rocks, same water, even same fish. But
the perspective is so radically different that you actually fish a new
river, wade into a parallel stream. What if you had not fished
upstream at all? Would it be a case of the river less fished, the piscatorial equivalent of one hand clapping?

Sometimes you need to hold a river up to the mirror in order
fully to understand how you should fish it. When I was a full-time

floats-and-leger coarse fisherman, moving either up or down-stream felt of little consequence; it was simply the direction one took to the swim of one's choice. If you trot for chub, roach or bream, then, if you move at all, you are more likely perhaps to fish a succession of swims downstream from your starting point, on the grounds that your loose-fed offerings will have drifted far downstream, and that if you move to the next swim down, having exhausted your own, you just might intercept fish moving up to locate the source of the free lunch. But there are few, if any, occasions when normal coarse fishing involves actually placing the bait significantly upstream of your location. And so, when you exchange wagglers for hoppers, stickfloat for stickfly, it demands a leap of faith to believe that the only way is up. If you have the right tutor, or are only experienced in chalk-stream etiquette, you will have had the technique impressed upon you, but it is tough terrain to cross at the stage in your career when one eye still checks the back cast. It feels tough when you turn around, face the flow and feel the weight of water on your wadered legs; it can feel intimidating, alien, like walking backwards or speaking bad French. The difficulty aside, your perception of how the river is laid out, how it behaves, seems so at odds with how you have seen the river until now. The truth is, of course, that you have looked but never seen, never felt the bright dawning of comprehension.

Spate rivers present their own difficulties – as John Bailey memorably characterised them they are 'thin' – there can be many square yards of water with not a fish, just barren, gravelled shallows populated only by minnow and stone loach. Unless you return at dusk, of course, when the bow waves of chub and trout, even barbel, will repopulate the void which existed before sunset. And so location is both crucial and potentially extremely difficult in a rain-fed river. By the late 1980s I had fished the occasional day with Neil on the Wiltshire Avon and the Kennet and found rivers with their own challenges – presentation, depth and spooky fish –

but location was never a problem. Ten minutes with polaroids and educated eyes were enough to find a morning's worth of prey. It felt extraordinary to fish a river where 400 yards, sometimes even less, was enough to sustain two anglers for a full day. At home, one could walk half that distance just to find the 10 yards of water worth fishing at the head of one pool.

I fished the River Ure on the Bolton Estate water in mid-Wensleydale for many seasons, and after four years steady progress – sounds, aptly, like the school report of a slow learner – I was confident enough rarely to catch less than half a dozen trout per session by searching the water in time-honoured method, but the trouble was, it no longer felt enough. It was a plateau, and, whilst I had climbed up some stony outcrops to get there, the foothills in the distance started to become more of a temptation. They demanded exploration and stopped just being a view passively to be enjoyed. I had the confidence from my glory days in the soft South at least to fish a fly upstream, to spot the leader dart away, or simply to stop, where I had first learned the basics of fishing the nymph. My mind was therefore programmed effectively enough to strike at almost subliminal responses, but it needed some more education to apply the whole technique to stony-hearted Yorkshire rivers.

I had read an article about how effective the leaded shrimp could be on the Ure. I had fished the shrimp as part of a team with my now beloved Yorkshire Spiders, but results had been patchy. What was clear was that the Spiders needed to be fished just sub-surface, not pulled down to the depths by the leaded fly. And anything that reduced the phenomenal pulling power of the Snipe and Purple was to be avoided. Purple's not a colour often seen in nature, but trout would grab the Snipe and Purple wherever it was placed on the leader. But it was not infallible and I needed more than this arrow in the quiver.

On a hot bright day in May I was scrambling through the shallows of a long pool on the Ure above Wensley – near Redmire, in fact (the real one rather than the pseudonym coined for that certain carp lake in the Welsh borders). At the head of the pool the water was studded with football-sized rocks, and the current swerved and curled around them, accelerating as it did so. The water was not deep, perhaps a foot or 18 inches at most, but it was ripple-broken, and I realised that this could be important on this shadowless day. I knew that trout needed highly oxygenated water, knew that the current would be washing down the occasional nymph and bug, knew that a trout could easily find sanctuary under the bigger rocks if shadowed by heron or angler. I could not fish the water from upstream, and I knew that if I even crept up from downstream into the tail of the next pool I would trigger a phalanx of bow waves as spooked trout arrowed their way to the deeper water.

And so I greased the leader down to within a foot of the Shrimp and I made the short cast upstream. The current pushed the fly line back towards me and I remembered to strip hard with the left hand to keep pace with the slack. Within a couple of seconds the leader straightened. I struck without conviction. Upstream fishing was not a viable technique in the north; it was clearly a rock or debris which had caused the phantom take. But it was, of course, the confident gulp of an opportunist trout living precisely where it should have, eating whatever good things the current delivered. All fish in shallow water – especially when it is clear too – fight hard and fast, and this brownie bulleted out of the current into the pool above, where it leaped repeatedly before I landed it in a haze of exhilaration. A good fish of over 1lb, dark-flanked and with full fins; not a stock fish, then. I noted how well hooked it was compared to the precarious skin-deep holds which the method that still not dare speak its name usually produced. I almost felt the scales start to slide from myopic eyes. Why had I not explored sooner? Complacency, once recognised, has a bitter flavour; it tastes of regret.

I wanted more of this, now. It felt like hunting, felt like targeting a fish in a place where it should be. Suddenly, the method which etc., seemed like playing battleships, seemed passive and dull. How often had I cast my team of spiders blindly across the stream, taking another pace before each recast, mind in neutral? And how often did fish even stay hooked? With my new technique I realised that I could probably catch six fish in as many casts if I used my intelligence and judgment. If I really started to hunt, rather than harvest, perhaps things could get a lot more ... intense? I thought about the apocryphal story of the young man being taught to shoot by his father, who gives son two cartridges and tells him to bring back dinner. This approach adds focus and risk but, more importantly, it frees up a whole lot of time to observe, to plan strategies and to work out tactics before taking the killer shot.

The observation point was crucial. On that same hot day I stalked upstream very slowly, eyes hard focused on every piece of likely water, anywhere that would be safe and comfortable for a trout. The smaller the area the better. Not only would it mean that a well placed cast would pitch the fly into the fish's window of vision, it also probably meant that a larger, more aggressive trout had played the natural selection trump card and staked a Darwinian claim on the honey pot. I had a wry sense of *déjà vu* – it felt like my first day solo with gun and dog.

I looked towards the left bank, which was heavily shaded by a solid line of willow trees. There was a fish; not the usual multi-ringed rise form but something far more subtle. A slight disturbance, the hint of a trout's dark nose turning slowly, confidently, to engulf another drowned beetle. The shrimp pitched into the river a yard above the rise. There was the tiniest hint of a vortex, and I lifted the rod slowly to move the sinking fly and immediately there came another confident, leisured take which I met with a quick strike into a bolting trout – another pounder. My too obvious thought was that I could very easily get used to this new style of hunter gathering; and more than that, there now could be no going back to passivity.

My confidence rose with each success. Fishing rivers upstream, searching for fish, inducing takes became addictive. It was hard, intense fishing, compared to the easy-minded neutral rhythm I had become accustomed to; the only thing I really missed was unrolling a long cast to the far bank. This new technique was all short range, stealth and sniper tactics. Accuracy and timing were suddenly not just necessary, but vital.

Weeks later I fished the mayfly hatch on the Ure many miles downstream. This was the water where I had fished for pike and chub for seasons, where I had caught scores of grayling in the autumn on trotted maggot or Snipe and Purple. I had caught a trout there too once, a perfect wild fish of nearly 2lbs and I took it on a lobworm intended for barbel. The water was managed by Brian Morland, a man utterly steeped in the natural history of the Dales and someone who knew his stretch of river at every level and in every possible sense. He told me there were small numbers of good trout, rarely caught, but worth fly fishing for at the right time. Which was mayfly time, of course, because nothing triggers fishy synapses like the cornucopia of a mayfly hatch. We did not have Kennet-sized hatches on the Ure; passing traffic was not arrested by the density of fly, but in a good year there was enough mayfly to trigger some gluttonous response from chub, dace and grayling. And trout too, I hoped.

I waded up a rocky 15-yard-wide pool. The surface was unbroken, but there was a clearly defined current swaying down towards me, marked by stippled beads of foam from the rapids upstream. Mayfly were blundering around, now that the hatch had started properly; it was mid afternoon. Dace and small grayling snapped at them impotently. I waded slowly and watched, and after five minutes I saw an assertive sub-surface swirl, looking like a sudden flash of sunlight between the clouds. I cast a mayfly nymph above the swirl; I induced a take and I caught a 2lb wild brown trout, followed, on the next cast five minutes later, by another of 1¾lbs. This time two casts had been enough. It was a good feeling. Perhaps I *could* become a sniper, not a machine-gunner?

Rubicon crossed, no looking back, now all I wanted to do was run down this new road to wherever it would take me.

CHAPTER FIFTEEN

NORTH

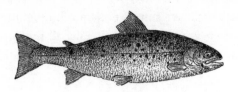

Great things are done when men and mountains meet

WILLIAM BLAKE, 'Gnomic Verses', i

SCOTLAND. WHAT WAS IT good for? I had played at salmon fishing, grown bored with big-loch pike fishing and did not rate the trout fishing highly. I had read the reports of the Aberdeenshire Don in *Trout and Salmon* with the same detached level of interest as I applied to reports of fishing for bonefish on the Caribbean flats or catching steelheads on Vancouver Island – where, I suspect, I would have spent more time on grizzly alert than fishing, timorous soul that I am. In the case of the exotic overseas venues I worried that they would devalue my home-grown sport; I had spent most of my life in territory where I had wonderful fishing within thirty minutes of home, and I did not want to tarnish its lustre by exposing myself to the bright glare of the Fraser River or Las Salinas. I knew anglers who had caught the New Zealand bug and kicked their heels between their annual trips, because their local waters now seemed so parochial, inadequate and dull. Steve McQueen's Michael Delaney character in the film *Le Mans* drawled 'Racing is Life. Everything that comes before or after is just waiting.' Glacially cool, of course, and a sustainable philosophy, so long as you can afford a competitive race car and have the time and money to compete in more than a couple of races a year. But I wanted to race every weekend if I chose, even if it was on my hillbilly streams, rather than on the piscatorial equivalent of Le Sarthe.

So the long-haul trophy venues were not for me. And as for Scotland . . . it just did not have enough to appeal. A 3lb wild brown from the Don on a nymph would have concentrated the mind, but I caught them nearly as big at home and in waters which I understood – knew – at every level. And although the learning itself can be good – wading up a small river for the first time feels like hearing your favourite band's new album – it can be unfulfilling and exhausting too, especially when it covers a whole holiday. Perhaps the big lochs would appeal – Ericht, Garry or Arkaig? Home of the *Salmo ferox*, and for me, like everyone who has read about them, they have immense appeal: the size, the fight, the location and those echoes of Victorian sporting tourists. But I knew enough about *ferox* to suspect that the reality was cold, hard days trolling into a deep void. I might start with a tank brimming with hope, but I would be running on fumes within a couple of days. Because fly fishing does that to you: makes you busy, impatient, drives you to catch fish regularly. I could not imagine waiting for a week for the chance of one take from a fish which probably didn't even exist. So *ferox* have remained another vicarious pleasure, with the exception of my brief encounter on Sionascaig described in Chapter Four.

I knew little about Scottish lochs, and that little knowledge was dangerous enough to condemn them: they were cold, barren, acidic and capable only of supporting populations of small-bodied, big-headed, poorly conditioned brown trout. In this Kingdom of parsimony, half-pounders were knights, pounders kings, and two-pounders myths. There could surely be no point, no pleasure in fishing such a Lilliput? But I did find the point, and I felt that first warm wave of pleasure when I spent a week in a small cottage overlooking Loch Hourn on the north-west coast. My parents loved the area, and had originally been drawn to it by its proximity to Sandaig, where Gavin Maxwell, of *Ring of Bright Water* fame, had lived with his otters and fought his demons. My drive along the Road to the Isles had enthralled me; Lochs Lomond and Awe had a tartan, clichéd beauty, but this wild country had a space I had never imagined could be present in Britain. How could this wilderness share a landmass with Leicester Forest East, Bluewater or Brixton? The road had been fast, smooth and as deserted as I might have expected in Utah or Patagonia. But not here. And as I drove high over the Ratagan Pass, Kintail and Duich to the east and Skye to the west, I knew I had crossed a boundary into somewhere I thought only existed in accounts of Edwardian shots and rods. The road, single-track and grass-encroached, stopped finally, emphatically at Corran, a tiny hamlet humbled by the mountains behind it and the sea loch in front of it. There is a thin, rough drover's road leading up into the mountains behind the village, and from the cobwebbed window of the cottage I could see Knoydart, empty and beautiful, and over the sparkle-blue ripple of Loch Hourn I could see the inclined silhouette of Rum. Even if the fish proved to be small, this setting shaded the familiar, made it seem impoverished, tame, lacking somehow.

The drovers' road was a tough walk, rocky and almost vertical in places on the long march in to the hill lochs, the lower of which had been raised by a Victorian dam. The silence totally enveloped me, harsh call from hooded crow the only sound to pierce this echoing tranquillity. There were no rises, no insects, no sign of life anywhere on this rock-barren loch. But it only took the one cast to undermine the first impressions; two quick stabs at the wet-fly team of Ke-he and Black Pennell. Both takes felt in the hand, but so quickly that I was able to react only to something which had already happened too long ago. Perseverance, more pacing the banks, more casts and I started to catch fish; lots of trout which were absolutely faithful to the expected norm. They were small, scrappy but utterly beguiling. Their sheer numbers and the setting in which they were caught made this addictive stuff.

On the walk back it started to feel like a Wagner opera; I have never been comfortable with thunderstorms, even from the safety of office or car. Trouble is, they feel malevolent, predatory, and the long odds do not always ward off the fear. I have been caught in several storms whilst fishing, and have never been more terrified; logic tells me that the odds shorten dangerously when you are alone in a treeless glen, and I cowered pathetically next to a rock outcrop and listened to the cracks and rumbles echo between the mountains. I lay almost prone, carbon rod discarded, trying to convince myself that I was not being chased by a jealous God, and I only succeeded when the clouds disappeared in the direction of Loch Quoich to the east; but the gold-skied sunset, with a view over the spiked majesty of the Cuillins to the west could have made anyone a believer. Slowly, I walked back to the cottage, and I counted sixty red deer en route; Grafham was never, *could* never be like this.

It did not take long to find other lochs; I was introduced to the factor on an estate near the Five Sisters of Kintail and was directed stony miles up an unsurfaced track to a larger loch of 50 acres or so. Mountains to the south, shallows to the north. And this water was completely different to the Corran hill lochs; it had weeded bays, rocky promontories and regular hatches of olive and buzzer which induced the odd slashing rise; the type of rise that does not come from fingerling browns. I suppose it was that biomass thing again – I suspected that the absence of feeder burns meant that spawning was difficult, and the few fish which lived here had less competition, more food and hence more weight.

The fishing was not of the three-takes-per-cast type any more; in fact I only had two takes all day, but both came from fish of over 1lb. But their memory weighed heavy enough to divert me from next year's planned trip to the Hampshire Avon, because I had to return north; I wanted to be intimidated by the mountains, deafened by the silence. And I wanted – needed – to catch wild brown trout in waters with unpronounceable Gaelic names, waters which had been populated by these tough fighting fish since the last Ice Age. Of course, I swallowed the romantic myth of the Highlands in the same way my predecessors did. We ignore the history of forced clearings, evictions to the Americas and we convince ourselves that the wilderness landscape is God's work and not ours. A little self-flagellation? Of course, just to preserve my liberal sensibilities, but not letting them get in the way of what I want to do. It's the dinner-party frown, a ritualised expression of one's humanity, made whilst discussing climate change or Iraq, but actually speculating whether the expensive wine that you brought is ever going to make an appearance.

Neil and Steve were – are – two very close friends from university days, and a decade's worth of postgraduate fishing had annealed a tough bond between us. We had the odd hissy fit – me especially on occasion – but we could navigate around each other's reefs and shoals like seasoned pilots. Three was a prime number which worked so well for us. I have always been an evangelist in fishing matters and had persuaded both that I had seen the future – trust me – and that it was fly fishing; my enthusiasm had been enough to hook both, and we agreed to a May week in Sutherland.

We had chosen Altnaharra because the advertisement in *Trout and Salmon* had so appealed to me. And the name was so fey, rolling over the tongue like a mini Haiku, albeit thirteen syllables short of the real thing. It seemed as though you could bank fish at Altnaharra too; we all had some nervousness about spending a week drifting some squalling loch, and we would have needed two boats because three men in a boat are a Bad Thing, but a single man in a boat would be equally bad and . . . the rest. And none of the other advertisements had ever mentioned bank fishing because, we assumed, it was not allowed. Poor innocent wights, we had not realised that no one had mentioned it because it was a given, no one bothered to fish the bank when there was a boat.

None of us had stayed in a pukka fishing hotel either, and as we drove north our apprehension was unspoken but enough to make us laugh a little too long, talk a little too loud; we must have seemed like conscripts before the NCO's inspection. But the further north we drove, the more genuinely exultant we became. I drove up the long hill from Ullapool, underneath the gorse-yellowed hillside reeking of that unexpected coconut smell, and as we saw the soaring bulk of Ben More Coigach, then Stac Pollaidh, Cul Beag and Cul Mor, we became breathless, hyper with enthusiasm. Loch Lomond had been pretty, Loch Hourn too, but this . . . this was like something out of Tolkien. None of us had imagined the north-west Highlands could have stunned like this; and, two decades later, I still can feel the same surge of adrenalin on the road to the far north.

The hotel at Altnaharra offered a degree of formality which was alien to us. We were used to the low-key pie-peas-and-pints routine of Wiltshire pubs on our barbel and chub expeditions to the Avon, but now it was a novelty to discuss precisely which wine we should have with dinner and to have to wear something other than moleskins and tired shirts in the hotel bar. It was not as though we couldn't do this claret-and-three-courses performance in our normal lives – we already knew how to hold knives and forks properly – it was that the formality sat so strangely with this remote location and our reason for visiting it. Even the remoteness was far more profound than we had expected. We had driven up to Loch Naver before dinner on our first evening, I had turned the Citroen's engine off, and we had looked south towards the great bulk of Ben Klibreck. The silence we encountered was deeper and more total than any of us had ever witnessed; there was no noise, anywhere, from anything, and even our breathing felt like an intrusion into this peaceful void.

We fished Loch Meadie on the edge of the Flow Country, a long, narrow-waisted loch, and although we spurned the offer of a boat – still angst on that score – we caught dozens of trout, easily. It was captivating, enjoyable sport but we were quick to realise that our capacity for this repetitive enjoyment could be finite. Predictability can shadow even the most productive day, but there was an easy solution: change the loch. So we walked out into that trackless waste between Lochs Loyal and Naver; we walked uphill through a misted emptiness and fished Lochs Breac Buidhe, Eilaneach, Staink and a chain of unnamed lochs further out on the hill. It was very difficult to read these waters. A small, weedy and shallow lochan might produce hard-taking fish of ½–¾lb, tail-walking through the stones and weed beds, but a bigger, apparently more appealing, loch would seem populated only by midgets. There were compensations, though; I saw an adder slide silently to the margins of a loch, bend its head and drink, black tongue flickering with unexpected delicacy, almost with grace, as if he were a connoisseur of waters. The snake had the detached, drowsy air of one recently awoken from a long sleep, and he slithered with slow, careful moves down through the rock and heather. I felt a bond, some sort of recognition, an acknowledgement echoing between us that we were somethings in this nothing, this wild country whose absences only served to define it.

Four days of hill loch bounty saw us content, but perhaps sliding towards sated complacency. We had not expected it to be quite so easy, quite so predictable, because most of our fishing holidays involved a degree of black-mooded despair, lost fish and missed opportunities; this was so perfectly according to script that we felt bit-part players in a Scottish *Stepford Wives*. Strange how a little disappointment can season triumph so effectively; strange how taste-free success could become. We had been sceptical about some of Bruce Sandison's comments on Highland lochs – were they all as full of breakfast fish as this cornucopia? It seemed as though they could be.

We drank our malt whiskies after dinner and consulted *Trout Lochs of Scotland*; we looked north and west, which is where we found the Cape Wrath lochs. Sandison's tone was different about the Durness limestone waters: he did not enthuse about dramatic baskets of fish, didn't recycle the same advice about how traditional fly patterns would suffice, but instead he described waters which offered big fish, averaging up to 2lbs but challenging, difficult and elusive. And even Cape Wrath's name would carve a memorable notch in the belt – it may actually mean 'turning point' but I prefer the sharper bite of anger in my interpretation.

I have made some journeys which, even as I experienced them, I knew I could never forget. Some for the wrong reasons, the journeys where you dread arrival because of what awaits you: dying parent, lover's indifference or the latest firefight in a war of arguments. Other journeys I remember for their exhilaration, the anticipation suffusing you as you count the miles to a longed-for destination. And I remember the joy of a fast, hard drive through France, 600 miles behind us, Vivaldi on the stereo and the Route Napoleon scrolling over the Alpes Maritimes, on a sun-gilded spring evening. But I remember, most of all, driving north on a soft-edged morning from Altnaharra to Durness. There was blue sky above, and the mist which had rolled in from the sea obscured what we knew must be majesty; but the sun beamed through, starving the darkness and killing the mist with a spring-hot light. As we drove along the single-track road along Loch Eriboll it felt like the curtains had been rolled back to reveal a brightly lit stage. Fantastically blue sea, yellow gorse on the hill and blinding white sand with ranges of barbed mountains in the distance. Behind us, to the east, we could see the impregnable fortress of Ben Hope and the spikes of Ben Loyal. We drove through Durness and noticed how the trees – one especially – were carved into triangles by the westerlies. And we found the Cape Wrath Hotel: a white sporting lodge on lush green turf, rabbit-scarred and peppered with wild flowers. The view south across the Kyle of Durness made our necks prickle – a sanded bay crowned by Foinaven, Arkle and Cranstackie.

Jack Watson, the hotel owner in the mid-eighties, greeted us, and he looked exactly as the proprietor of a hotel on the edge of Europe should have done. A Scot, of course, reserved, polite and with a schoolmaster's gravitas – which he would often subvert with a twinkled smile. We booked a boat for the following day and we walked down to the slipway where the ferry leaves for Cape Wrath itself (the place where, nearly two decades later, Joanne and I would watch an otter devour a flatfish with crunching relish a short 4 yards away). The ferryman was doing the sort of stuff which men who know about boats do with boats. It is activity, but its purpose is often difficult to fathom; you suspect that the activity is actually the objective. The ferryman looked like a Celtic highwayman, wore a yellow duster around his neck – of course – and he spoke in an accent which was utterly alien to us. It was singsong, lilting, sounded more like a Welsh-domiciled Swede than a Scot. We did not know all the words he was using but we immediately understood that this place already felt like a new home.

CHAPTER SIXTEEN

THE OTHER PLACE

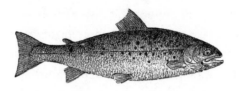

Three fishers went sailing away to the west
Away to the west as the sun went down

CHARLES KINGSLEY, 'The Three Fishers'

PERHAPS PHILIP AND BILL had it right all along. They were a piscatorial item at the Cape Wrath Hotel; both were retired, one an ophthalmic surgeon from Edinburgh, the other a teacher from the north-west of England. Philip was bird-like, ascetic and reserved, and he stalked the banks with diligence and stealth; Bill was burly, opinionated and impatient, but his bluster failed to cloak his love for the Cape Wrath lochs. Philip and Bill fished Loch Borralaidh (Borralie) almost exclusively, and only rarely did they bother with a boat, letting the fish come to them instead. You would see them, 20 yards apart, sitting on the high grass bank as cattle grazed around them. They would sit well back from the water's edge, and they would watch the hours and days away. Borralaidh is as clear as air, and the littoral shallows reflect the light in a pale yellow band. As it deepens, yellow turns to green and, deeper still, as the loch sides angle down, green becomes tinged with brown; further out again, brown darkens into an unfathomable deep blue. Philip and Bill had learnt that the fish would appear from the deeps and patrol the green/brown border, where they would truffle shrimp from the limestone-rich bed or intercept olives, sedges or buzzers as they twitched towards the surface. Philip and Bill did not fish blind; they were not playing the game of chance with Black Pennell or Peter Ross, but instead they fished small dry flies and targeted individual fish as they moved up against the wind. Some days I suspected that neither Philip nor Bill cast at all, but their good days could see them take six or seven fish averaging up to 2lbs; and I doubt whether they took more than ten casts to catch.

Croispol was a loch which changed our entire approach to boat fishing. Because it was one of the very few lochs where bank fishing was restricted to a limited area, we reluctantly accepted that the three of us would have to share the boat, taking turns to row. The experience was a revelation: not only was it a superbly social, companionable way to fish, it was also infinitely more successful than two men in a boat. We had not realised how important it was to have a twenty-minute break from casting every hour, how vital the oarsman's role was in positioning the boat just so at the start of a drift and, once under way, maintaining the drift by deft short strokes on the oars. We realised, too, that fishing can be a spectator sport, especially when you know that you are the one who is really responsible for putting angler over fish. Participation by the ghillie includes the important things – netting, hooking, weighing, counselling – and the mundane – untangling leaders or rowing an aching-armed ten minutes against a buffeting south-westerly. And on Croispol, location was so critical. It is a small, rich loch, heavily weeded and with very few deep voids. Our first day there was the sort of day which fly fishermen are supposed to dream of; there was a moist south-westerly wind, enough to create a rounded unbroken ripple on the loch. The sky was heavily overcast but the day was warm, and the air had the soft density which stimulates fly and fish. Olives hatched, and as we rowed down to the southern end of the loch they looked like little matchsticks spearing through the surface until, in a confusion of movement, they were transformed into duns, newborn on the surface.

Watching the olives change from nymph to dun made us realise why wet flies can work so well; nothing seemed to us better to represent that tangled movement of transformation than an Invicta, even the colours seeming faithful to the original.

Steve on the oars, Neil and I stroked the water with wet fly; we had not yet learnt the dibble but a gentle retrieve was enough as fish after fish jagged into the flies. They were big fish by Scottish standards, if not by Cape Wrath's, and they ran to 1¾lbs. And limestone fish have a solidity, a fitness and a sheen which humbles most acid-water fish, but Croispol fish were pre-eminent. They fought with a toughness which came close to madness, and, even in death, their shapes had a perfection of proportion and colour which can make even this agnostic admit to the possibility of a god, or, more accurately, the need for one. We may be pro-grammed to recognise the perfection, but it only takes one whisky for me to ask when, by whom and why?

Fishing Croispol in the eternity of a June evening, when dusk eventually becomes dawn without intervening darkness, was unforgettable. We had watched the rabbits play on the east bank, and we had heard the corncrakes clicking to each other on the wild-flowered pastures. *Crex crex*, an onomatopoeic Latin tag for a bird living on the edge, in every sense. We had seen a polecat sliding with quick-stepped malevolence in that strange hovering light of an evening in the far north. And the fishing was utterly extraordinary, as if daytime fish had been replaced by an even wilder race. They were hard-bodied silver trout, sea trout in every sense but the literal, and they fought with a violence which both stunned and exhilarated. Takes would come out of nowhere; gone were the soft, confident taps and draws of our afternoon idyll. Instead there were savage, slashing takes which broke more than one wind-knotted leader. The fish ran, leaped, ran again, before sounding under the boat. Rod tips were dragged under water – and this from fish that only rarely exceeded 2lbs.

Caladail is the most conventional loch: large, open and shallow. Its western end is bisected by sunken stone walls, across which a boat might scrape, breath held. Beinn Spionnaidh lay to the south and Beinn Ceannabeinne to the east; to the north was a sliver of land and a lot of sky, arching over the steel-blue grey of the Atlantic. Halfway down the south bank is a stranded boulder the size of a small car, probably discarded there by the last glacier to retreat, millennia ago. The rock looks like something from a Salvador Dalí painting, creating an impression which outweighs substance because, in that landscape of absence, it could only be pre-eminent, because centuries had passed since it had itself been shadowed by the Caledonian Forest. And I cannot count the hours I have watched that rock: sometimes distractedly, as another drift starts on a viciously bouncing wave, sometimes almost with affection on a still evening with a soft lopping swell, with buzzers hatching behind the boat and with huge, oily head-and-tail swirls exploiting the bounty.

Two fish I remember more than any others from Caladail. My first and biggest limestone fish was caught on the stolen day from Altnaharra, and it came on an aimless drift in mid-afternoon when retrieving a Black Pennell on autopilot. I hadn't seen or heard a fish for hours, despite conditions being apparently so perfect, and I had retreated into that dangerous reverie where you seem to be fishing but are, literally, going through the motions. Until, unforgettably, I was playing a big trout whose silver and gold reflections semaphored up through the green-tinged water beneath the boat. A long hard fight; hands shaking, heart pounding; 3lbs 5ozs – and it outshone a score of hill loch trout.

A couple of years later Steve hooked his big fish on the same loch on a cold, glowering day with an edgy wind from the northwest. The waves were aggressive, jolting the boat in a hard, slapping rhythm with their wind-driven solidity. There are some days when even though conditions are not right, they are not entirely without hope either, and you can grasp on to just enough confidence to ride through the day. This was such a day; we had caught a couple of 1lb fish, missed the odd rise, and even in the confusion of waves rolling past us we saw the occasional tell-tale flat spot as a fish cruised just under the surface. Steve was fishing a small Dunkeld, having convinced himself, rightly, that most of the food items on the loch were small, and that our flies should be too. His rod tightened suddenly into a fish, and he backed into the weight; I stripped my line in and stowed my rod; I retrieved the drogue just as Steve's reel started to sing with a quickening rhythm. No long, theatrical scream, just a steady, determined run outpacing the boat in the green and blue waves. The run carried on; 30 yards, 40 yards, 50. The fish did not do anything dramatic; it was focused, determined, and it just kept on keeping on, in the words of the country song. After ten long minutes we landed her, one ounce over 3lb, the boat bouncing hard against the rocky shallows of the eastern bank, almost a quarter of a mile from where Steve had hooked her.

Borralaidh is Cape Wrath's Koh-i-Noor: it has a lustre which outshines all its peers. I think it is about proportion, size and colour. The loch is big enough to be unknowable, yet only really intimidates when a force-eight southerly comes screaming up the Kyle, fuelled by the barren slopes of Strath Dionard and provoked by the crystalline peaks of Arkle and Foinaven. The sky has a proximity and a depth of colour which only the endless Atlantic rollers can conjure, and on a calm night on the loch you can hear the deep rhythmic sigh of the waves immediately to the north. The eastern bank of Borralaidh is sheer, crowded in by rocky cliffs, modest in height but enough to make an angler fishing at their base vulnerable, insignificant. Most of the banks are rich, soft grass, so much in contrast to the acid heather wasteland to the south and west. It is living geology, and you realise just how much this soft limestone can give to land and water. Every stone in the shallows seemed populated with shrimp, caddis and writhing little olive nymphs; there is an extravagance of life here.

Borralaidh has a large island which on the eastern bank almost makes landfall, so narrow is the channel. And the island can shine a muted purple in the late spring, when the wild purple campion blooms around the hatching terns and gulls, and on the banks there are wild spearmint and yellow iris. With a morning-fresh blue sky above, few places can feel quite so life-affirming, especially when you are slowly drifting towards the island from the dark, deep water towards the triangle of shallows immediately to the south of the shore. As you see the first columns of rich weed appear out of the void, it feels like breaking through the cloud on an airliner's final descent; there is a relief and a mounting, urgent sense of anticipation.

In the evening, the light on Borralaidh can be utterly extraordinary – this far north the sun describes arcs which are alien to most of us. Although the light will start to fade at ten, the sun does not so much set as dip below the north-western horizon for a couple of hours. The view south from Borralaidh over the distant white building of the hotel is dwarfed by the mountains bordering, and then finally punctuating, Strath Dionard. They shine with a red-gold glow, and when the peaks are flagged with stubborn belts of surrender-white cloud it is hard to say anything intelligent to your boat partner; instead you nod southwards, exhale audibly and shake your head in wonder. It was on such an evening, with an almost exaggerated languor that Jon and I rowed the boat silently up to Half Moon Bay, halfway down the western bank. There is a wide expanse of shallows there, and the trout love to explore it when the shadows lengthen. On calmer nights – and this was one – you can see the shoals of char stippling the surface, having risen from the blackness they inhabit in broader daylight. Watching char is like seeing the light from a dead star: an echo of something long ago, when Scotland first emerged from the ice and these cold-water fish first populated the glacier melt.

Jon and I had fished hard already that day, and our cheeks were burned bright from wind and reflected sunlight; arms tired from casting and rowing, we fished out our casts slowly, wondering whether the calm would last, or whether one of those late evening gusting winds would assault us from nowhere, then stall completely and restart ten minutes later from a point diametrically opposite its first fretful sally. But tonight it stayed calm, and trout moved slowly, deliberately into the bay. I cast 15 yards and let the long-leadered Buzzer freefall over the shallows before a so slow, so gentle lift of the rod tip twitched it to the surface again. When it came the take was unmissable; the whole fly line moved slowly, deliberately north-west. There are moments in fights with good fish when you just have to pause, to hard-wire the image to your memory, so you can replay it in years ahead, when you will smile vacantly and realise that your eyes cannot focus on your surroundings but can only recycle images from the past. This was such a moment. The fight was long, but my confidence, whisky-fuelled, was well founded. Not 3lbs but very nearly, and as perfect a trout on as perfect an evening as I expect ever to experience. Jon died five years ago in a car accident just north of Scourie, on a road I drive along on each visit to Cape Wrath; it is a poignant feeling, but an hour on Borralaidh makes me remember the special times too. There is a bench to his memory overlooking Half Moon Bay – a good place to sit and to reflect.

Cape Wrath is a name that carries serious resonance, and, although the eponymous hotel lies in a green oasis, it is surrounded by a heather and rock wilderness, stippled white with cotton grass. Across the Kyle lies the Cape itself, reached via an 11-mile military track. The ascent from where the ferry lands feels like a vertical take-off, and the views to the east, over the Kyle towards Durness and Eriboll are incomparable. Some destinations are

programmed into nearly every soul – Paris, Florence or New York
– whilst others are more personal. It can feel like there is some sort
of imperative to go there, and, until you make the journey, the
lack of fulfilment can make you ache with regret. Cape Wrath was
like that for me, and until I first crossed the Kyle I had never realised how it was much more of a need than a mere destination. We
rattled and bucked in the tired minibus which plies the loneliest
road in Britain, and, as we reached the first brow and the full
majesty of it all sank in, I wept silent tears. Don't know if Neil and
Steve noticed – if they did, they know me well enough to have
tacked around my emotional rocks.

Cape Wrath lighthouse stands there, hundreds of feet above
the Atlantic. The last time I stood there was on a hot May dawn
in 2003 watching the eclipse of the sun as it appeared above the
north-eastern horizon. I had never expected to see the Cape
crowded, but on that dawn it felt like praying in an open-air cathedral with a full congregation. Fishing the Parph, as the Cape side
is called, can involve big walks and small fish; in that respect it is
a mirror image of the limestones, with their easy access and
shrimp-fattened trout. But the Parph's setting is wild and edgy
enough to sharpen every sense, to make you feel you have done
something you can feel proud of, experiencing something which
you know you will bank in your memory. It becomes an invest-
ment to spend on reverie, when the bad times won't go away.

One year we walked south over quaking peat bog and heathery
slopes to a sprawling loch called Airigh na Beinne. No trees, except
in the tiny burns sheltered from the wind, where bonsai rowan
and birch scraped a slim existence. The burns contained tiny trout,
and in an autumn spate even the odd grilse will thrash its way
through the peat-stained dark water. I do not think we counted
the fish we caught from the loch that day during that holiday; it
felt like a stolen midweek afternoon from work, so much had the
limestones taxed us, punished us for our presumptuousness. We

had become used to a take being an event, and a missed one, a near tragedy, yet in this bouldered emptiness we caught trout after trout. Never big, perhaps ½lb at most, but fishing together so companionably, for fish whose capture or loss was almost insignificant, and in a setting of such grandeur was simply joyous.

We had heard about Loch Keisgaig in the hotel bar from two guests; their generation has now almost passed (this was the 1980s) but they epitomised the Cape Wrath Hotel guests back then: upper-class, or upper-middle at worst, with the social ease which a public-school education seems to guarantee, military precision and a total absence of the self-deprecatory lack of confidence which so many baby boomers can reveal without having to make conscious efforts to compensate. They drawled assertively that they had fished Keisgaig, uh, was it about thirty-five years ago? As if it could have been last week. They told us of the walk in, the size of the fish and the setting, and we were hooked. Back then, thirty-five years ago was a lifetime – literally – but, now that another twenty years have passed, the thirty-five-year reference feels a little more sustainable.

We walked in across Maovally bog, and the sky, although bright, had that depth of blue scarred with white clouds that suggested the weather would soon break. I fear nothing other than flying, thunderstorms and too many everyday occurrences to list here. I admit it, on some days, from my house panphobia can be seen in the distance, waiting to pounce. Neil, knowing this, failed to share the forecast he had heard that morning. The loch was exquisite, though; shallow on the north, deeper on the south under rising rocky hills. The bays had coarse red sandstone beaches, and you could sense the Atlantic a mile to the west as it rolled into the Bay of Keisgaig. Casting a fly in this water felt like much more than fishing it, felt like divining a meaning from this chaos of water and rock. Few spawning burns, therefore few fish, but the trout we did catch were tough, hard fish, up to 1lb. Their heads were bigger than the limestone fish, and so were their tails – great dark spades to spear the fish back into the depths. It did not thunder, but the black skies above meant that it could have, and my walk back across the Hill was with the strides of an Olympian.

I have not returned to Keisgaig, and now I should admit the possibility that I may never do so; I hope to be in a position to say that I did fish it thirty-five years ago, however. But I have returned to Cape Wrath, to the limestones, and to that view which lifts my heart.

The Other Place? It became such an obsession for us that we had to work hard to convince ourselves that we should ever fish elsewhere in the Highlands. The name had become a siren call luring us back year after year. And so it became The Other Place.

CHAPTER SEVENTEEN

ASSYNT

They hear a voice in every wind,
And snatch a fearful joy

THOMAS GRAY, 'Ode on a Distant Prospect of Eton College'

FURRED BY THE CAPE Wrath limestone, we headed south for the hard rock of Assynt. Although we had not fallen out of love with Caladail and Borralaidh, we were too young to settle down. Fly fishing demands such promiscuity, and we needed to see Cape Wrath through another prism, to evaluate its worth against more conventional Highland fishing. Actually, 'conventional' is not really the *mot juste*, as it would demean the majesty of the setting of Assynt, where each mountain seems to compete with its peers for grandeur. Too tough a call to decide whether the ramped incline of Quinag outshines the surreal twin peaks of Suilven or the spectacle of Conival, but I do know that to encounter them all in one territory can soak the senses.

Bruce Sandison had provided the pornography – as usual his gleeful trousers-on-fire enthusiasm was infectious, and, whilst he is rarely muted, he reached new summits of hyperbole in describing Loch Veyatie, Little Loch Awe, Cam Loch and Sionascaig. Admit it, it is near impossible even to say Sionascaig without lingering over the syllables, angling your head north and affecting a whimsical, unfocused smile. Especially when you have fished it yourself . . . been truly Out There. And you carry its memory like a talismanic stone in your pocket, to be touched in the bad times like an agnostic's rosary. If you have a copy of Sandison's first book on Scottish trout lochs, look at the jacket photograph – I did, months after our first visit to Assynt, and I felt that unsettling shiver of *déjà vu*. Of course, it was Sionascaig; but the missed heartbeat came from the fact that I had taken almost exactly the same photograph from the same point halfway along the northern bank.

The last time I stayed at the Inchnadamph Hotel I was on a touring holiday, *sans* fly rods, with Joanne. I had told her about the rough-and-ready hotel miles from anywhere, with its public school dinners and its Victorian charm, told her too about Willy Morrison, the soft-spoken proprietor, who was either painfully shy or very dour – I never quite could decide which. But Willy had died by then, and we saw his grave in the churchyard down by Loch Assynt itself, a place where the words 'rest in peace' were as literal as they were metaphorical. The old hotel had passed on too; the new version was snappier and offered – unprecedentedly in Wester Ross I am confident – not only vegetarian main courses but also that essential adjunct to Highland living, the trouser press. I looked forward confidently to the valet parking and the video conferencing suite. I should not complain too much, as Inchnadamph could feel a joyless place to stay in the eighties. It had a feeling of parsimony, a leaden formality, and it felt crushed by its surroundings. But how many hotels have a map behind the bar impaled with black pins showing the locations of fatalities on the hill – to add a touch of drama to one's postprandial whisky? And how many can offer the sight of a golden eagle from the car park, or a herd of red deer ambling over the pasture 50 yards from the dining room?

We were used to a degree of choice in where we fished our Highland breaks, and we were more amused than nonplussed on our first day when Willy drifted over to us after breakfast, frowned at our Marlboros and suggested that we needed what he termed a wee pipe-opener. If only on etymological grounds, there was no choice other than to assent to the Assynt ascent. Pipes were duly opened, if not completely rebored by the combination of endless uphill trudge and clear mountain air. Below us the view of Loch Assynt looked like a Victorian sporting print; above us the massif of Ben More Assynt appeared and reappeared through the mist. We arrived at a loch which we agreed to treat as Gillaroo Loch; it had been a long walk, and who would know if it was not? The real Gillaroo was so called because the Victorians had decided that the existing natural strain of fish needed spicing up by the introduction of the eponymous trout from Ireland. We did, of course, catch some trout, but they seemed no different from any others on the Hill. It seemed to us that the pipe-opener was some sort of initiation ceremony as, having done as instructed, choices started to become available at every breakfast briefing.

Loch Borralan was one of the stranger lochs to fish; it is a fairly uniform oval shape, next to the main road and really rather underwhelming. Whilst the surrounding countryside suggests that this would be a deep loch in places, an impression its dark peaty water does nothing to dispel, the actuality is very different. For here was a loch where it was possible to jump out of the boat and lead it on its rope through the apparently abysmal depths, a hundred yards out from the shore. We left God-fearing believers to draw their own conclusions at the sight of man apparently walking on water. Borralan's other incongruity was its hatch of mayfly, admittedly a month later than their chalk-stream counterparts, but still the real *Ephemera danica* deal. Steve had convinced himself this was the loch upon which he should learn to dap, and he quickly learned that, far from being the appropriate method for lads and ladies, as it was termed half-wittedly in one of my older trout fishing guides, it was actually a very challenging method indeed. Whilst takes were easy enough to induce, with half-pounders hurling them-selves out of the water to drown the fly every few yards of each drift, connecting with them was something else again. We guessed that it was to do with the size of fly – enormous – and the size of fish – not enormous. The experiment had proved the method worked, and we could return to the deadlier trio of wet flies we had now adopted – Black Pennell, Invicta and Dunkeld. How ironic that we were the ones who had so wanted to believe every new wonder fly which appeared in the monthly magazines. We were the ones who had consigned dry flies to history's dustbin and regarded traditional wets as the province of uninformed old men.

We flirted with Little Loch Awe, a compact version of its namesake in Argyll. If you were tasked with writing a specification for a small loch, your design would look something like Awe. Variety: islands, indented shoreline, weedbeds. Accessibility: five minutes from the road. Fish: plenty of brown trout, many big enough to put a satisfying degree of bend in the rod. And, in autumn, there is the chance of a grilse – but isn't a chance often all that is necessary in this sport of hope?

A confession. I started to write about Little Loch Awe because its beauty merits a few hundred words, and if you have driven past it you will have done that head-swivelling fisherman-reflex routine. But I am not writing a tourist guide, and so I will be honest; the only thing I remember about fishing this loch is missing lots of takes, and becoming progressively more tight-lipped about this. Not really a memory to cherish. But I do keep one image – and sound. We were drifting through that Highland silence, profound enough to make you look up when you hear a car approaching on the road above you. We heard the music first: it was something operatic, and it was played at full volume through the open window and sunroof of a car heading north. Rods were clipped on the roof, and I knew I was watching a very happy man, travelling hopefully and perhaps praying that he would never arrive – because what could have been better than this? So it is what I witnessed from Awe, rather than my experiences whilst afloat on it, which still carries any weight. The truth is, if Center Parcs made a risk-assessed, family-friendly Highland loch, it would look something like this. It is a kid's TV presenter of a loch – and grown-ups like me prefer a Mariella Frostrup growl to a girl-band simper; we notice the woman who walks from the hips, not the knees, the woman who is a strider and not a stepper. Because what you are *like* is what is important. And Awe did not feel like it could kill you, just for fun, just because it could, just because your insignificance meant you could never really matter. Awe felt a tamed loch in an untamed wilderness.

But nowhere felt more like a stalking murderer than Loch Veyatie. Not a loch that you should fuck with – at least not more than once, because once is the only chance you would ever get. Veyatie is a long, thin loch scarring westward towards the coast through country which has been emptied, *is* empty. All that is left is water, rock and great rolling cubic miles of air, salt-freshened by the Atlantic. So you can breathe there, breathe like you never could in Manchester or Potters Bar, and you can see there – you really can see for miles and miles and miles.

I have a book called *Wade the River, Drift the Loch*, by R. MacDonald Robertson; picked it up for a tenner in a second-hand bookshop in Thirsk. It was published in 1948, and it chronicles the wild sport of the north-west. My favourite chapter is – inevitably – 'Angling in Remoter Sutherland', illustrated with a picture of a doughty cleric called Walter E. Lee, Ph.D., of Perth. In his arms he cradles a cast of a trout he had caught from Veyatie in July 1938; it weighed 16lbs and was 32 inches long. The Reverend's Ghillie was Murdo MacDonald of Elphin – even the supporting cast in this Highland microcosm had names which are simply unimprovable. And it is so easy for me to close my eyes, remember my day on Veyatie and then think back to that scene fifty years earlier, as angler and ghillie battled this monster of a trout near the Black Falls of Veyatie. Romantic? Damn right.

The sixteen-pounder had been caught in a strong westerly, but we had a hard howling wind from the east blowing us westward down the loch. We had heard from another guest at Inchnadamph that outboards were available for the asking; they had never been offered, even on a foray out on Assynt itself but, once requested, a motor was immediately produced from the hotel shed by the redoubtable Willy Morrison. And did we need it – the easterly was enough to ripple the water in spiked peaks 20 yards from the lee shore, and a mile down the loch the boat had started a lovely rolling canter of a drift. Neil, Steve and I had refined our three-man routine to perfection by now, and we had learned to shadow the steep banks within easy casting range, rather than aimlessly drifting over vacant depths. I remember the boat drifting under an oatmeal sky; I remember how I had learned that a few well-timed caresses on the oars were enough to present my two anglers to the cliffs rearing up on the southern bank, and I remember how we forgot how many fish we caught that day. It was probably a hundred; and every single one felt twice as big as its 4 or 6 ounces as it crashed and leapt through the rolling waves. It was the sort of day which leaves your face glowing, half deaf from the roar of the wind and with a memory overloaded from a blizzard of images. Brown buzzards winging over heather waste, raven's call echoing over scree slopes, red-throated diver cleaving the waves like a newly surfaced submarine, constellations of jungle-green fern starring a night-black cliff and boat bows crowned by white spray. And if ferns look like the first plants, we felt as though this was the first loch and we were the first men. Apart from Walter E. Lee. (Did he think again of his mighty trout on his deathbed? Would you? Would you expect your God to offer you such bounty in your heaven? I would, and on a wild grey day in the far north-west from a killer of a loch like Veyatie.)

And finally, inevitably, I must return to Sionascaig. Do I try to describe how it felt on our first trek down from the Inverpolly road? Of how she looked that first morning, cloaked in solid white mist until suddenly, startlingly, the ridge of Stac Pollaidh reared into view like a stegosaurus, and Suilven's twin towers looked like a mountain from a Kipling story? Of how we drifted towards the yin and yang of Cul Mor and Cul Beag, crowning the eastern horizon like brown pyramids?

All these images make up Sionascaig's DNA, but there is an even stronger one, which none of us who were there could ever erase. It was the sort of July day the inexperienced tourist expects to turn into the perfect summer's day. There is a south-westerly breeze, warm and thick, and the sky is a deeper blue than you dare to imagine. If you have fished the Highlands in July you know that this is just the cheerful overture to the *Sturm und Drang* symphony that follows. We were spared – thankfully – the *Donner* and the *Blitzen*, but the black clouds had grown fat as they rolled north-eastwards across the Atlantic. The sun was hot enough to steam off a previous shower but we knew the next one would drench even harder. We had taken shelter in a forgotten bay with silver-grey water slapping hard into the moored green boat. Canopied by overhanging peat hags, we shared our dry haven with a seething cloud of midges. We drank coffee, sipped whisky, we smoked and we talked. For once it was not the talk of hope, of how the next drift would be better, how the fish would be larger and the rowing would be easier. Instead we talked of how we had first noticed this long, U-shaped bay facing south-west and how the wind had created a white-foamed calm lane, slicked flat and holding what-ever terrestrials had made their last mistake in the storm-confused wind over Sionascaig.

We had drifted into the bay three, four, times already, starting at a point 400 yards out from the shore where we could ride the lane into the tightening bay. Each drift had produced violent, stabbing takes from trout cruising with intent just below the waves. On our last drift we tracked close to the shore on our final approaches, close enough to see the black rocks protruding like sea stacks from the waves. Only 2 yards in front of the rocks, but still over deep water, the wind lane's slicked surface was broken by the silhouette of a feeding trout. Steve cast perfectly – two feet in front of where the fish had shown; he drew the line slowly over his left hand and he lifted into a trout which was one of the most beautiful fish we had ever seen. Yellow-flanked, black marbled, and with a tail of rayed perfection, a tail which belonged to a fish of twice the weight. This fish had a presence which nearly twenty years have not erased. The record book will say 1lb 2oz, or something equally prosaic – but the impression, the memory, transcend the mere numbers. Because the Best of Times are really beyond measure.

CHAPTER EIGHTEEN

FINESSING THE POOL

*Now my charms are all o'erthrown
And what strength I have's mine own*

WILLIAM SHAKESPEARE, *The Tempest*

P
RIMUS INTER PARES (FIRST among equals, if your Latin lies
rusting) – that is what this chapter must be. The tough fact is
that it has to carry the key theme of the whole book and to do this
it needs to be wind- and water-tight; if it isn't there will be daylight through the roof and hailstones on the stairs. The difficulty
does not really lie in the subject matter, small-river fly fishing,
because it is something which I really do rather well. Or, expressed
more modestly, it is a branch of the sport at which I am less inept
than many others. I will never be a good pike nor carp fisherman,
but I can fool myself into believing that I am a capable fly fisherman, and sometimes even a good one. Finessing the pool is the
term I use to describe how to conjure fish out of places they should
not be; it can be a feat of skill, but has a close acquaintance with
sleight of hand. In its ultimate manifestation, it can feel like

catching fish which did not even exist until your fly created them. Metaphysical stuff? Oh yes indeed.

Of course I could compress this chapter into a snappy précis which would read something like 'build your confidence; nurture it; apply it' – or, even more simply, 'confidence catches fish'. All this is true, but the much more interesting exercise is in finding out how you build the confidence, and, once it is constructed, how you let it influence your fishing and where you will let it take you. It is not enough to possess it, you need to work it hard, to exploit it. And there are choices – do you allow this confidence simply to evolve by a Darwinian approach, trying ever more methods and allowing natural selection to identify the most efficient? Or does that have something of the chimpanzee-writing-*Hamlet* times-cale? Maybe you can allow some redneck creationism into your life, perhaps you could allow inspiration to create a faith? The truth – or at least *a* truth – hovers somewhere between sharp-edged pragmatism and pure spirituality, but the latter is more fun, more unpredictable and ultimately a lot more rewarding.

You may already have noticed that this is not a technical book, not one full of diagrams of knots and casts, nor patterns of flies so lifelike that they become ends in themselves. Too anal for me, and such flies have a formality, a stiffness, which has no natural parallel. And here might be a good place to own up to the fact that I do not even tie my own flies. (Pause for weight of ghastly admission to sink in with stunned reader.) Look, I used to build Airfix kits, but I wasn't very good at that either. I abhor DIY, and I would rather pay someone to paint my house than waste a weekend doing a worse job myself. I am comfortable in my lack of practical ability, and I have never accepted it as a part of my sport. It is not, in the same way that writing about it isn't. (Writing is something which is complementary, something upon which to exercise your brain, to sharpen memory and to refocus forgotten thoughts. It doesn't make me a better fisherman, just a more verbose one.)

And so the nuts and bolts of fly fishing are not terribly important: they are just physical means to obtain whatever fulfilment we crave when we fish. If my Hardy Sovereign were to snap tomorrow, there would be frowns and F-words – but, hell, no one would have died. It would not have been a tragedy, there would not be a wreath at the roadside, nor an obituary in *The Times*. A small exception might have to be made, however, in the case of my twenty-six-year-old soft-action Diamondback. We have become rather an item, I confess, because we have been adventuring far too long not to have borrowed a little from each other.

But, Diamondback apart, rods are not pets, they are not even as alive as an old sports car can feel, with its oil and petrol reek and its exuberant backfires. Rods just perform to a standard, and when they do not you simply buy another one. But a good rod should be able to fool you into thinking that you are playing a fish only through blood, sinew and bone. Reels and lines should be a given, just media through which you reach your prey, and they only became important when they are no good, and that is the only occasion when I spend a little time thinking more about tackle rather than tactics.

So this finessing business is not about what you buy but more about what you should think, and how you should fashion a faith muscular enough to achieve what may at first seem unknowable, then unrealisable and ultimately a revelation. In Chapter Fourteen I wrote about how the change from fishing downstream to fishing upstream could feel like holding a mirror up to the familiar, and in this chapter the mirror is again the key. But this time it involves not a physical reversal but a mental one, where the impossible can be transformed into the achievable, the difficult to the straightforward and the absent to the present. Not something often written about in the angling press I admit. This can be a high-wire act, and the truth universally acknowledged is, of course, that you should never look down. Nurture the confidence, never look back

either, never doubt . . . and some days you may find that fish –
taking fish – can be everywhere you want them to be. If it works
well enough, the perfect moment comes when you start to suspect
that what is creating the fish is your skill, and that they would not
be there at all without it. Is it a performance, a McKellen or a
Gielgud delivering lines which transcend their provenance by the
actor's delivery, emotion or nuance? Or is it a variation of the elemental trick of water into wine?

At the start of every season I get that dry-throated dread that I
will not be able to do this alchemy any more. In the winter, I will
have looked down from the high wire, started to wobble, begun
even to doubt. Never fallen yet, but the fear of falling is almost as
bad as the fall itself. I might have felt like Prospero at the peak of
his power last September when the catching of fish had become
almost a formality, but then the magic became just another piece
of winter kill. But I do somehow manage always to recreate it, and
I cast the first tentative spells on cold, hostile days in early April.

So this is what I have learned about river fly fishing – that it is
an art more than a science, knowledge that cannot be taught – and
this is how I learned to believe what I know.

The first glimmer of the great enlightenment happened during
my early days of river fly fishing. I was on a day-ticket stretch of
the Swale, which, although primarily a coarse fishing venue at
Morton, could still offer enough variety in depth and flow to make
fly fishing more than an affectation. I had fished this stretch since
university days for chub and barbel, and I had a mental map of the
swims which were worth fishing. Almost without exception they
offered far-bank bushes, even but not rapid flow, and a depth of
three or four feet, and preferably more. I caught fish from such
spots because they were where I fished – and I fished there because
I caught fish from them. This self-perpetuating confinement could

have continued for years, as even the most innovative fisherman is snared by the familiar, made conservative by past successes, relying upon them as a passport to the next one. The only reason this inertia did not continue was that I arrived on the river on a July Saturday in the early 1980s and found a dozen cars already parked with their occupants fishing the swims I had intended to target. At that stage I was still drawn inexorably to the familiar, and I could always catch a few trout and grayling from what actually was good barbel water and mediocre fly-fishing water.

My chances were narrowed further when I realised that there was a match in progress on the far bank. It had been pegged intelligently, missing the shallow runs (which were obviously fishless), and concentrating on the more alluring water with greater depth and cover.

At this point the Swale is a narrow river, and, even though I could have fished opposite the matchmen, I knew my presence would not have been welcomed, especially if I had waded to midstream and rolled the fly line over towards the far bank. So circumstances forced me to fish the shallow runs between two steep and featureless banks, offering neither cover nor shadow. The river ran in a straight line for several hundred yards over clean gravel, occasionally punctuated by small patches of weed. This might sound attractive enough, but my confidence was flattened by the fact that hardly any of the water was more than a foot deep and most of it ankle-deep shallows.

It was clearly lifeless, fishless water under the high summer sun, but I fished anyway; fly fishing running water was still enough of a novelty to make practice essential, even if the prospect of success was virtually non-existent. Except, of course, it wasn't. The water which had looked so barren actually harboured shoals of dace, grayling and small chub, which attacked the wet flies with enthusiasm. Take after take came from what, short minutes before, I had dismissed as a fishy desert. I caught a dozen, fifteen fish, none big but enough to attract the occasional ribald comment from the matchmen upstream as they watched my rod arch over yet again into another fish. And, on a light-action fly rod, even a 4oz dace produces a convincing bend. If one of the matchmen had hooked his hoped-for big barbel or chub, it would have far outweighed a score of my lightweights, but there was no doubt who was having the more fun . . . who was concentrating harder, fishing better and being rewarded for doing so every couple of casts.

There was something going on here. I didn't know quite what it was, but there was clearly a phenomenon, even if it was, as yet, impossible to understand or analyse. I felt as if I were an uninvited spectator seeing something secret, privileged and mysterious. On the surface, literally and metaphorically, all was as before. But beneath, in another dimension, I knew something different was going on. Reader (now sighing with weariness at the metaphysics), what the hell was going on? How to deconstruct all this stuff? I was sometimes catching fish from habitat which I had summarily dismissed as having no potential at all. Fish surely had no business being there; how could a dace or chub live in 6 inches of fast-flowing water and not be seen, nor do anything to betray its presence? I was staggered at this development, and the ground which had seemed so solid was now so shaky. I was catching fish from places where they should simply not have been. Not just fish which I knew little about, like grayling, but my beloved chub too. It was truly a revelation, and it has transformed all my fishing, not just fly fishing. Maybe it is the hunting gene; in most coarse fishing you create a trap, an inducement to feed by loose feeding or ground baiting. It is skilful, technical sport, but it relies on a different mindset to the fly fisherman's. Your best chance of catching a fish with a fly is always – always – the first time it sees the fly. If it recognises it as something that probably should be there, possibly good to eat, looking plausibly similar to a nymph it ate a moment ago, the fish will calmly, confidently breathe in the fly in the same way that you idly transfer another peanut from packet to mouth. And so I came to realise that not only was there something to finesse, but that the more I applied my mind to the admission of possibilities outside my experience, the more I would succeed.

The River Laver is a small tributary of the River Ure in North Yorkshire, and I first fished it on a hot midsummer day, the time of year when you begin to realise that the season has already peaked. The leaves looked tired, dusty, and you start to crave the fresh wind and rain of autumn. That year I had fished the wider streams of the Ure and Swale far too often, and I hungered for something more difficult, more intimate. The Laver is a hidden gem of a river, running east to Ripon from the low foothills of the Pennines. Its lower reaches are limestone-rich and alive with wild trout and the occasional grayling. And, unusually for Yorkshire, the water is available on a day ticket. Both its accessibility and the very different environment it offered made this too tempting. I had become a little blasé about the bigger rivers, thought I had cracked them, understood them – although hindsight reveals that all I had achieved was a scraped pass in one subject.

I swore a lot on my first day in the Laver; the combination of a 9-foot rod – the Diamondback of course – canopies of willow and alder and my inability to cast in any manner other than the conventional overhead, made me a bumbling duffer of an angler. I lost flies, I smacked the rod tip into unseen branches; I stumbled like a lost heifer through shallow pools, and my eyes grew tired from retying new leaders. I sweated with irritation as I fished upstream, and even that was a novelty for me.

I concentrated on the spots where I saw fish move; usually those deep, mirrored pools with only a suggestion of a downstream flow: the type of territory more suited to chub than trout, a habitat which sees fish idly dimple the surface, sipping tiny smuts with leisured ease. On the comparatively rare occasions when I neither spooked the fish nor cast a fly into the leaves, I did tempt a few fish to show interest in the fly. No down-and-across rod-tip thump, but sudden short stabs of the leader which were almost impossible to hit.

I managed two or three trout, unremarkable fish except by their means of capture. But the scale of my defeat, if not full-scale rout, stung me so hard that I just could not leave this as a disastrous first date, and I knew I had somehow to make this relationship work. It felt as though I was stepping out with a spiky, haughty mistress, but I had once seen how she could smile and I was besotted.

Consummation had to wait, but eventually it came on the River Rye, the scene of my first clumsy flailings with a fly rod in university days. It was fifteen years after I had left Leeds' Faculty of Law, but the Rye was still enchanting. At Nunnington the river runs fast over bright, clean gravel between green wooded banks and under the huge sky which crowns the Vale of Pickering. Upstream, where vale tightens into dale, the valley can be tight, dark and almost threatening, but here the atmosphere was always benign. There was streamer weed swaying in the current, and the better pools could look like the Kennet. I was still in my nymph-fishing phase. (It lasted far too long and it was a struggle to shake off. Its appeal had something to do with embracing the iconoclasm of Sawyer, Walker, Ivens and Church against the pomposity of Halford and his counterparts. All nonsense, of course, and attributable to the simple fact that I still had the chippy attitude of the specimen hunter, hard-wired to despise tradition and mistrust convention.) I fished my nymphs better now, and as I cast my hare's-ear and pheasant-tail nymphs to rising fish, I started to learn the code.

Deep pools still produced fish, but I became much more daring when it came to fishing faster, shallower water. I realised how a fish could hang over the gravel with minimal effort, darting up periodically to grab a nymph or bug brought down by the strong current; I started to understand that if a fish stationed itself in fast water it had done so deliberately to feed, not to relax, not to hang out with its shoal mates.

I caught a lot of trout on the Rye, and big grayling too, and the confidence became a tangible thing. I cast into water that a season ago I would have splashed through, having dismissed it as too shallow, too fast or too exposed. Fish started to appear, apparently out of nowhere, as if the method were not just catching the fish but creating them.

Hold on to that thought, because it is the key to the finessing game, and let me wade up another tributary to consider Schrödinger's Cat. No, I had not heard of the Teutonic mog either until I read a piece in the *Independent* which rather beguiled me. The feline experiment is actually – gosh – about quantum mechanics, and so you can understand how I cannot always make up my mind how relevant this is to fly fishing, although after two glasses of Shiraz it can feel like the key. It is about a cat in a box, and the box also contains a phial of poison which may – or may not – have been activated. And the point is this – until the box is opened, both possibilities – purrs or *rigor mortis* – have equal weight, the same validity; neither can be disproved. The cat's demise depends upon the state of an elementary particle and the cat, just like the particle, is actually in two states, both dead and alive, until the box is opened and the contents observed. A good fly fisherman always opens the box, and there is always a live cat there – or so you should believe. Or something like that. Or perhaps Stephen Hawking was right; he said that 'Every time I hear of Schrödinger's Cat, I raise the sights of my blunderbuss.' But what does Hawking know? If he is unaware of the fact that a blunderbuss has no sights, the depths of his ignorance must know no bounds.

I moved on to the Cod Beck, a tributary of the Swale, which is smaller, deeper and much less attractive than the Rye. But it is even richer, and the fish are bigger, fitter, stronger. Some came from the conventional spots, but many others came from what had been the unexpected locations but which were now turning into the predictable: rippled streams, tiny tongues of calm next to a tumbling white-frothed current at the heads of pools, slivered runs probing hard against alder roots and apparently barren ankle-deep stickles.

The dry fly started to appear on my leader. Having long dismissed it with the arrogance of the ignorant as some sort of party trick technique, I had finally begun to accept its place. A growing awareness of river ecology helped: I would see how a warm April sun would trigger a flurry of hatching dark olives, see how the trout would be stimulated into action, walloping the duns from the surface. Whilst a nymph might still have worked, how could I so deliberately ignore the obvious? And so I started to experience the exquisite satisfaction of watching the artificial fly float downstream, cocked just so and with such a silhouetted realism that I knew the take would come where and when it did.

The fish were just as firmly hooked as on a nymph and the average size was bigger. I found a practical advantage in the dry fly too; a badly cast nymph, especially a weighted one, would usually be irretrievable from branch or bramble. But dry flies parachuted down with such delicacy that not only could they be extricated with ease, with a little extra technique they could be fooled into landing in parts of the river which had previously been completely inaccessible. You know the type of spot – the 8-inch gap between the long grass and butterbur on the far bank, the spot where you have seen the tiny vortices that betray the presence of a big trout, staked out in his own little kingdom.

Until a cold east-wind morning on the upper Rye, I had always fished a dry fly to fish that were either rising actively, or at least were visible. Nymph fishing still felt the most natural way to explore a river blind, as I did not yet believe that dry fly could induce takes from uninterested fish, the trout which are present but not really engaged. The deep-cut valley of Ryedale ensures that spring always comes late to the upper reaches of the river, and even now, in early May, there were only hints of green from the trees at the head of the pool. The water was cold, and the sky had that hard grey uniformity which so often is the product of an east wind blowing off the North Sea in spring. Light levels were not high, but this was a more open pool, and there was enough bright-ness to ensure that my Iron Blue looked irresistible as it glided down the main current towards me. Like many fly fishermen, I have actually encountered Iron Blue only rarely, but the Plunket Greene who exists in all of us makes it almost imperative to use this fly in an act of homage to the Bourne.

There was no natural fly on the water this early in the day but, so long as I cast the artificial to where I felt it could convince, I managed to catch trout. In fact, in two hours I had caught fifteen fish up to almost 1lb. Whilst I knew I might have caught almost as many on the nymph, I knew they would not have been the same fish; they would have been smaller, less satisfying, and I would not have caught them from the places where the Iron Blue had cast its spell.

Later in the season there should always be days – usually in late June or early July – when, if you keep the faith, you can catch fish from almost anywhere. Think of them as Schrödinger's trout (existence entirely dependent upon your enquiry). Inevitably I am on the Rye – of course, there is no more gorgeous trout stream in Yorkshire – and this time I am in the tight-shouldered valley above Rievaulx: a place whose memory can lighten the darkest of black-dog December moods. It's warm, perhaps 19 or 20°C; there is a moist wind from the south, gentle enough just to disturb the leaves at the tops of the trees above me. The water feels warm, too, but with a pace and a clarity which is still fresh, a legacy from the big rainstorm three days ago. The light drizzle is not the irritant that it could be in another season, it is the sort of moisture which I know won't develop into a storm, or even a shower. So I wear a shirt and waistcoat, no waterproofs, because it is a summer evening, and I am happy enough not to care.

I fish a brown Klinkhamer into the evening and I ignore the obvious locations, because fly fishing should always be about the overlooked, the less apparent, the less cast over. The bats have started to wheel through the flies hovering over the river, and I watch the 9-inch-deep shallows 10 yards above me, rock-studded and usually so barren under the glare of full sunlight. Almost too subtle to discern, there is a tiny movement below the bigger rock, a tail's tip briefly cleaving the surface. A good cast – two months of the season instil a lethal accuracy which is now almost taken for granted – and I lift into the fish immediately. It is a full-tailed brown trout of 1lb, and it crashes through the shallows with an anger which is palpable. Play him down to the net, unhook and return his glare. We live in parallel universes, and this moment will probably be our only contact – discomfort, perhaps even pain, for him, and the opposite for me. Wonder if there is another parallel universe where I am the one who eats the flies and he is the one who drives the Golf and drinks Laphroaig? Shudder; then return to my own reality and inch upstream to where there is an almost vertical slide of water over sharp-ridged rock. It is all cross-braided currents up there, perhaps worth a pitch with a pink shrimp on an October afternoon for a grayling but not with a dry fly, not in that turbulent confusion.

But what about over by the black water at the edge of the current, where the ferns grasp so tightly into the fissured rock? It is only inches wide, a foot long, and shallow inches deep, but tonight I know that all could be possible. Fly bounced off rock, rod tip held high and slack line thrown to avoid drag. The fly has disappeared – drowned or taken? The bucking rod tip tells me which.

The final pool is far more open; the sky has cleared, and there is a soft afterglow gleam on the water. I do not know if there is a fish in that fast, shallow ripple, but I do remember how big trout in dark streams love to lie in the light. There is not a rise now, but, as the fly emerges from the alders' shadow upstream, it is visible briefly before the evening's biggest fish engulfs it. On virtually any wild trout river a fish of a 1¼lbs is – should be – a fish to treasure, and this one is not an exception.

These vignettes illustrate how I progressed from timidity to confidence on the trout streams and rivers which I have come to adore. To begin with, I was on a gentle stroll, so mundane were my expectations and my results. But now, on a good day, it can feel like mountaineering without rope or compass. I stopped being reluctant to try the obscure, the unfathomable, the near unfishable. I can finesse the pool with a fly, and I can catch the unexpected and, on a good day, almost the absent. If I ever still think about the river as a downhill flow of water and mud and rock, I have missed the point. But if I let the river transcend its physics, allow it to become alive, mischievous, devious and generous, I can again understand that strangely engaging line in John Fowles' *The Magus*. The narrator is asked 'Which do you drink, the water or the wave?' Fly fishermen should always drink the wave, even though it is transient, even though it can seem to exist only in their own perception. Have faith in the wave, accept that what you see is not important, and that what is important is how you see it.

Postscript

I am not a teller of jokes; so brightly does my verbal dexterity shine that my services as an advocate have only rarely been sought. But I do need to share a joke (possibly the only one?) about Schrödinger's Cat; and before I recount it you will need some advice on the correct response to make on hearing it. A thigh-slapping, heel-kicking performance would be *de trop*. A more ironic response is needed – a short percussive bray, uttered at a volume sufficient to be audible in a full theatre. It's the 'Uh-Huh!' you will hear from two rows behind you during a performance of *Henry IV* or *Hamlet*, and it's made after some laboured *bon mots* from Falstaff or Rosencrantz. It is the laugh of recognition, the badge of the smart-arse, and I will confess to uttering it myself at appropriate points in plays by Tom Stoppard (our greatest living playwright – I will brook no argument).

The joke? Of course ... A play has been written about Schrödinger's Cat; the audience sits rapt with anticipation on the first night. The lights dim, the curtain rises. And the play ends.

CHAPTER NINETEEN

THE SHADOWED LIGHT

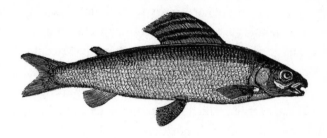

Between the idea
And the reality
Between the motion
And the act
Falls the Shadow

T. S. ELIOT, 'The Hollow Men'

THERE ARE A FEW obstacles that prevent grayling being my favourite quarry of all – sadly all insuperable. Problem one: they do not quite grow big enough. A 2lb grayling is a fish to covet, to be proud of, but it can never quite make the same impact as a 5lb wild brown trout. I have caught neither – so far – but I have come very close to the 2lb grayling on so many occasions that I am beginning to suspect there is a divine conspiracy which ensures that, yet again, Aston snatches defeat from the jaws of victory. But if I caught the two-pounder – and I would be overjoyed – it would not alter the problem; 2lbs would be wonderful but what I really need is the prospect of a monster, and 5lb grayling are in short supply in the United Kingdom. And even hope needs to operate within a vaguely reasonable framework if it is to sustain you.

Problem two: their season is too short. Summer grayling are, I admit, quite unfairly maligned – after July they are regaining their condition and fight with enough vim to focus anyone's mind. But they peak in winter, when, although fly fishing is possible, somehow it is just not what I really want to do. I have fly fished the Tees in January ice flows and sub-zero temperatures and I have caught grayling, but really just to show that I could, rather than because it was what I really wanted to do. As I will describe later in this chapter, a winter day's trotting for grayling can offer enormous satisfaction, which is close to the kick of a big grayling on a light fly rod – but sadly not close enough.

Problem three: their habitat is localised. To many anglers they are as exotic as an Arctic char, if not a burbot or a sturgeon. Of course, they are repopulating some rivers as the purges of the industrial past are transformed into historical footnotes, and the upper reaches of even rivers like the Don and the Calder now have sustainable grayling populations. But you just are not going to find a grayling biting your casters on the Sixteen Foot Drain, the Royal Military Canal or on any of the thousands of lochs in the Highlands.

But let me park the problems out of sight and concentrate on why the grayling is such a glorious fish. No argument, they are the most exotic-looking freshwater fish you will find in the UK, not just because of the obvious exuberance of their huge dorsal fin but because of the beauty and symmetry of their silver-mailed flanks and the impossible nuances of colour which can flash across them in the light of a winter's day. They pull hard, not in the three-laps-of-the-pool-and-a-double-leap style of a rainbow, or the dogged belligerence of a brown, but in a determined show of absolute resistance to being bossed around by anglers. Hook a big grayling in fast water below you and the first walloping thumps on the rod tip are enough to excite the most blasé of anglers.

The grayling's initial reaction to being hooked feels like a barbel, or even a big eel, as they just refuse to give an inch without making you work for it. And even when landed they will not concede that they just might have lost the fight, because they continue to struggle; holding a freshly landed grayling can feel like trying to control a cat in mid-tantrum.

Debate over. They are a beautiful fish, and I adore them, and this is what it feels like to hunt grayling on a winter's day. There is a kind of melancholia that runs through winter grayling fishing, the days are far too short, and this angler can find nothing to lighten the gloom of a prematurely black evening. I dread the inevitable cold, downward slope leading to the winter. In Philip Larkin's words 'it deepens like a coastal shelf'. And my mood plummets steadily between October and mid-January, when I start to admit the possibility that the reliable miracle of spring might just recur. But even in winter there can be hope, not just hope of the short but intense fishing sessions to come but also hope for the rebirth of the river in a few months' time. I love to anticipate the bright April mornings, the sun on my back and the smell of wild garlic on the wind. And when those days come you don't stop looking forward; and you keep looking forward until the end of September – when you are finally forced to look back, and you keep on doing so until, with profound relief, you throw away the Christmas cards, burn your pagan tree and once again count the days until April.

Angling is a sport which has to survive on hope and reflection to the extent that living in the present can often feel difficult. The problem is that the present is always too ephemeral properly to appreciate: you need to learn how to experience the present by savouring its aftertaste. As in the case of every emotion which carries weight, looking forward to rehearse the moment, or looking back to remember and relive it, is what really counts. Angling literature has exploited the cliché of winter being about roaring log fires (why do they always roar? Why not sizzle, spit and smoke like mine?), the good malt whisky and the fishing journal or the Skues to reread. Is that really what we do in winter – feet up like pensioners, complacent in our inactivity? If I really want to reflect, I tread the bank of a November river, and on the right day I will come home with a sense of absolute peace and a thousand-yard stare.

It was the last week in November, and I was in Bilsdale, up on the North York Moors. It's close to home and there isn't a mountain in sight, just soft rolling hills scarred by deep river valleys. Very little rain here, as the Pennines to the west steal most of the great depressions which roll in from the Atlantic. The rivers of the Moors are small, and Americans would call them freestone (I do not, of course – I prefer to characterise them as rain-fed rivers that rarely spate). If you choose your river carefully, you will find the water enriched by limestone, which produces the alkalinity to ensure a diversity and abundance of fly life. But even on the richest limestone stream there are slim pickings in late November.

Today a benign ridge of high pressure had moved in from the North Sea, 40 miles to the east, and the sky had the patina of old pewter, dense and immobile, ten-tenths cloud and no wind. It was the sort of day when a distant shot from a twelve bore sounds uncomfortably close, and when the raucous cackle of a jay or magpie can sound like the Beast itself hovering at your shoulder.

My last visit to the river had been with a fly rod, but today there would be no upstream nymphing, no opportunist fishing with dry fly during the brief hatches of olive, but a downstream search of the river with Trotted Worm. By the way, the technique deserves the initial capitals because it is not only a difficult method, it is also one with an honourable history in Yorkshire. Whilst float fishing a worm would attract frowns, if not actual unpleasantness on the Test, the Ebble or the Great Eau (Lincolnshire's little-known but delightful chalk stream), trotting is a long-accepted part of the Yorkshire angler's armoury. And if pitching a dry fly on an inch-perfect cast to cover a June trout is not always easy, neither is presenting a bait 20 yards downstream in low light or a turbulent winter flow. Unlike trout, grayling do not rush around the river, ferreting from side to side to intercept anything appearing edible; grayling do not like even to move laterally across the flow. Their preferred style is to hover on or very near the bottom, pear-shaped eyes focusing only on what the stream is about to bring them. When they see a fly – or a worm – they will rise in a deliberate, near vertical ascent with rarely more than a few degrees of lateral movement. So not only do you need to know which pool the fish are in this week (and they can move around like silver nomads), you also need to figure out exactly where they are lying. Because if you are a foot out of line the most you can expect is a disdainful shrug from the grayling's elegant shoulders.

So many generations of Yorkshire anglers – T.K. Wilson, Reg Righyni and the inimitable Walbran – have fished for grayling in waters like this that I felt almost as if I had a weight of ghosts accompanying me on the walk down to the river. But it was a joy, nevertheless, to stroll through the dense, cold air, and when I arrived at the river bank the gravel was hard from the previous night's frost. The air temperature was hovering at 2–3°C, and the river felt just as cold; it slid downstream like molten lead. I do love the density of a river's winter current, where the tiny eddies semaphore the rocks on the river-bed, and I love the sibilant conversation of the flow over the shallows, muted on this winter-calmed day.

A week ago there had been a big flood in Bilsdale, and new debris festooned the alders. The sandbed had been brushed clean by the flood but was already scarred by passage of birds and beast – roe deer, otter and mink.

I had to cross the Rye to reach its main tributary, the Seph. I waded thigh-deep into the cold dense water and exhaled involuntarily – Christ, but it was cold. I climbed the far bank and walked upstream, briskly, before finding my first swim. The river was wearing its winter *alter ego* – in summertime this would have been a pool but you cannot trot a pool, only a swim. In Chapter Fourteen I talked about the difference of perception that upstream fishing demands and creates, and now, years after taking the first step upstream, I had to relearn what had been so difficult to unlearn – to fish downstream. Here the river was 8 yards wide but it narrowed to a quarter of that at the swim's head. It was overhung by alders and had a brisk pace down the middle with a lovely crease dividing current and backwater. In the summer, even fishing with a leaded fly I had never hooked bottom when fishing this swim in its pool manifestation.

So I plumbed the depth – 7 feet – and most of this river is knee-deep. And how etymologically satisfying it was to plumb the depth in a literal sense – look, lawyers are paid to be pedants. My expectation level was high, because the swim was manifestly a grayling arcadia and my first cast saw the red-tip float course down the current, skid sideways into the eddy and inch back towards me – without a take, or bite as I should properly term it. And thirty minutes later I had still not received any response from the pool. There was trouble in this grayling paradise; 'alles ist verloren' as Marlene Dietrich would have put it (always assuming that she had developed a grayling habit). And so I stumbled downstream, and experienced the sheer unwieldiness of a 12-foot rod in a river meant for a seven-footer.

The next pool surely had – must have – grayling potential, but subconsciously I suspected that this was trout terrain. When you're a grown-up, illicit sport can seem a nasty, guilt-ridden business because, instead of teenage kicks, there is just regret and shame. I cast, the float disappeared immediately, and an aggressive little out-of-season brown trout charged around the pool. It felt like playing with a kitten on a string, and it made me grow up quickly. I realised I should have looked for a swim, not a pool.

I walked down to the junction with the main river and experienced a bout of indecision and irritation at my lack of success. I have never belonged to the school of fishermen who hold that being outdoors can be enough, that the catching of fish should never be a given, but a bonus. Whilst I might love the environment of the river above almost all other things, it is ultimately peripheral to the bite, the fight and the capture. Only then do the flora and fauna really delight – but they provide context more than focus.

My mind wandered . . . ironically I had spent too much time during a long meeting the previous day dreaming of when I would be thigh-deep in the cold river hunting my grayling in solitude, and, as if to punish myself, I had started already to rehearse the arguments for Monday's negotiations. I know that golfers do this all the time – there has to be some reason for their sport – but to me it felt like sliding into another Groundhog Day without a lapse of memory between.

I needed action to banish this introspection and I followed the river downstream to a pool which had promised so much in those exquisite months of May and June. It had delivered too, and while it only rarely produced a big trout, it did produce hard-fighting, 8–12oz fish in the peak of condition.

With a smile now unfocused I remembered how good it felt to see the dry fly disappear into another swirling vortex on the edge of the current. I remembered, too, how on a late August afternoon I had lain on the high bank opposite and I had marvelled at the slim, long shadow on the gravelled river-bed. This far up the river, trout are ubiquitous and dominant, with grayling elusive but of large average size. The French esteem the grayling and call it 'l'ombre' – the shadow. We English used to call it the 'umber', but this was superseded by the prosaic 'grayling'. That impossible combination of silver-and-lilac flanks capped by the orange-and-black marlin-like dorsal deserves so much better. I guess that

Thymallus will have to do, but I have to say grayling never smelled like thyme to me; they smell only of clean rivers, cold water and wild fish (but that should be enough for anyone). And, despite the glory of a grayling's appearance out of water, when you are looking into the water, they become near invisible – sometimes all you see is a telltale shadow which might be attributable to a trick of the light. Today there was no light and I only had a hope of catching my shadow.

I put a new redworm on the Size 12 barbless hook and made a perfect trot down the far bank, the float riding the flow perfectly over the 4-foot depth. The float did not stop, it did not stab under the surface but it folded gently over, exactly as if, not for the first time today, the hook had tripped the river-bed. I struck by instinct, with neither hope nor conviction. And then there was that glorious visceral solidity, impossibly heavy in the winter flow. The grayling bumped the rod tip over again and again, so unlike the frantic runs of the illicit brown trout. I saw the flash of silver, semaphoring through the green-tinged water, and I savoured every stab of the rod against the grey sky as I manoeuvred the grayling over the net. And there she was – all grayling seem feminine to me – outrageously pretty and a glorious 1lb 12ozs. Not a small fish for a little river like this one. I held the grayling up to what light there was, and I can still remember the cold, steely weight, the flamboyance of the dorsal and, most of all, the patrician glare from the haughty snout. If I wore a baseball cap I would have whooped. But my cap was tweed; it did not display the legend 'John Deere Tractors' or even 'Bradford Bulls', and, even if I had owned such a cap, my self-consciousness would have reduced my whoop to a whisper.

By now the sky had darkened to a tired sepia, and, although one fish is never enough, today it had to be. All rivers have a rhythm, and this one's beat is frantic in the summer when the living is easy for both hunter and hunted. But in this November half-light the beat was slower but more complex. This grayling was no ephemeral spark of glory but something much more profound. It was the secret to lightening the darkness.

CHAPTER TWENTY

BACK FROM THE BASEMENT

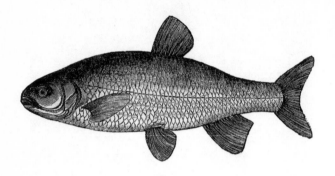

The Right Honourable Gentleman is indebted to his memory
for his jests, and to his imagination for his facts

R. B. SHERIDAN

MORE CONFESSIONS; WHEN I started to write the first chapter of this book I did not know it was going to turn into a book at all; it felt like writing just another 3,000 words for a magazine. The manuscript lay on my desk, untouched, for five years until 2005. And then I started to think about how long a journey I wanted to take, and whether an article would be too much of a stroll when what I really needed was a trek. I did not have a destination in mind, just knew that I wanted to travel far, take in enough good scenery en route and walk around some places, meet some people I had neither seen nor even thought about for decades. I am not blessed with a retentive memory; I tend to edit out everything which seems unimportant, and I obsess about what is left. I write like this too – I start with a huge bonfire of material, and I burn it down until only the hottest embers remain.

And so what you have read is what is important to me, what made me remember things which were felt hard or deep enough to have left an impression, sometimes even a scar. Fishing has been a way of life for so long that, even if I no longer fish as often as I used to, I think not only about fishing, but I think *as* a fisherman. This sport has become so much a part of me that the mindset, the skills and the self-containedness that it creates have made me view life through a piscatorial prism. But if this has happened, so has the reverse; light from my other *personae* keeps angling back through the prism, highlighting and shadowing my days on the river in sun or in cloud. (This sun, incidentally, is not – I hope – the setting sun which Viscount Grey sees illustrating the past peaks of his sport, but if it is still not yet sunset, the days seem shorter now, and on some mornings there is a cold mist hanging over the river.)

The looking forward will come later; I will try to end on an optimistic note: looking into the spring sun . . . that sort of thing. I can't have my audience leaving the theatre heads down and sobbing, this is not meant to be a tragedy but an entertainment.

But now . . . now feels like the end of a long climb up from the basement to the top floor, from where I am enjoying the view the elevation offers. On the climb up I affected a vacant smile for the people and places I revisited, then honed the memory which they triggered, added some half-truths and seasoned the text with some *ex post facto* rationalisations; hindsight can sharpen the most unfocused image, can transform hunch into insight or chance into choice. But I knew that already; it is the author's visa, it passports you into any destination without the inconvenience of border crossing or baggage checks. What I had not expected to find were a few hostages still waiting for rescue, ransom still due. I may pay a few off – but where will they go now? Will they want to live in my house? But some can stay and wait out the long years, captives of my forgetfulness. When I write again, you might meet them, but now you can read about the unshackled thoughts, blinking and rubbing their eyes in freedom's light. Having gone back to come forward, as it were, here are the differences between whatever was then and whatever is now.

The first and most fundamental truth I have liberated is that things are better now than they were then. There are plenty of negatives – a whole herd of the buggers jostling for position – but the inescapable fact is that rivers are cleaner in the twenty-first century than at any time since the industrial revolution. When I was a child, it was beyond my comprehension – and my elders' memory – that anything could have survived the poison-slicked water of my local rivers – the Aire and the Calder. Tales of how salmon used to run these rivers had as much relevance in the 1960s as the fact that dinosaurs used to blunder down the hill outside my village. And, while I doubt if many anglers in Leeds or Castleford yet elect to double-Spey-cast a Silver Doctor to salmon fresh run from Goole or Selby, the idea is vastly more credible than the prospect of catching a gudgeon or roach from the same river forty years ago. And I have seen salmon in the Trent, seen them head-and-tail in the Ure and watched them crash out of the Tees like great silver missiles.

Leeds doesn't have dirty-handed industry now; its streets are prowled by silver Porsches and black Audis, and the hardware shops of my youth have been superseded by the glittering retail sirens of Harvey Nichols and Vivienne Westwood. The shoppers might not notice the river uncoiling through the city, but the industries in which they work do not create the great seas of pollution which destroyed the life of the river for centuries. Accountants, lawyers and IT consultants certainly make an impact, but it is the more insidious spectre of global warming they have conjured, the consequences of which vary according to whether you dare believe the Gaian theory of a self-healing planet or whether you see news pictures of shrunken glaciers and thank your

God that your house is 600 feet above sea level. Or at least mine was, at the last high tide.

In the countryside of North Yorkshire, the changes are subtler, and they are not all good. Our industrial revolution was a short-lived boom of lead mining and ironstone extraction, whose echo had dwindled to near silence by the beginning of the twentieth century and whose remnants are now brown-signed industrial archaeology. So our rivers have had a long period of peace, with just the occasional violation by sheep dip or agrochemical spill to spike their quality. The Tees was nearly destroyed by pollution in the early eighties, fish and fly choked by chemicals carelessly spilled, but rivers are tough, you cannot kill them – or, if you succeed, they just recreate themselves whenever the conditions allow, like the dry seeds in the desert exploding into life after unexpected rainfall. Pollution can be like a flash fire, flaring high one minute and gone the next, or it can mutate into the *status quo*, the dangerous time where even the fighters give up because . . . well, it just is.

The more insidious threats to my streams come from abstraction and land drainage works. The former will be the real killer, reducing flow rates, destroying spawning grounds and increasing concentrations of toxins. The latter is simply municipal vandalism carried out by organisations whose principal objective seems to be to justify their existence by perpetrating ludicrously ill-thought-out schemes. Their drainage improvement works have no clear purpose and are carried out with no awareness of, nor responsibility for, the appalling damage which they create. You know the sort of carnage – banks planed to a uniform 60 degrees, grubbed-out gravel beds, chain-sawed trees, and whole habitats destroyed. My local internal drainage board has waged its own petty war on a favourite trout stream for decades; it rationalises its work by claiming it is reducing flooding in the local market town. But, if it achieves anything, it is to deliver the maximum volume of water in the shortest time to the next pinch point downstream, which is – entirely predictably – a road bridge in the said town. *Quel surprise* – more flooding. But also a justification for obtaining more funding to carry out even more vandalism. The drainage board cuts down the alders and willows, and a year later the bank collapses and the contractors are sent in to shore up the bank with piling. The same bank that had held fast for years, thanks to the network of roots from the trees which the board has destroyed. And I am paying for this lunacy; I am paying these bastards to grub out otter holts and destroy the nests of sand martin and kingfisher.

But, the drainage board aside, my local streams fish far better now than ever they have. The words 'in living memory' would not be appropriate, however, as the old boys in my local club still wallow in the nostalgia of some lost golden age when the rivers had more, bigger, better trout than now. And when confronted with the evidence – in the form of my Honorary Secretary's records going back to the mid-nineteenth century – they refuse to accept it. You know the poem about the old cat, losing his touch, complaining that the times seem to be breeding a new strain of faster, smarter mice? Enough said.

On my ascent from the basement, I have also realised how few fishermen there now seem to be, at least on the waters I fish. In a typical winter I fish for chub and pike on perhaps a dozen occasions, sometimes more. I fish some syndicate water, but mainly day-ticket club water accessible to all. And this last winter I saw one other angler; I had literally miles of water entirely to myself. Some of the swims looked as though they had not been fished all season, as even in late autumn I needed to clear a way to the river through thistle and Himalayan balsam. A decade ago I would usually encounter a handful of fishermen on each trip, and often would not be able to fish at all on Sundays, as entire lengths would be match fished. Where have they all gone, and why did they go? They went to the small commercial fisheries, and they fish them because they are easy to fish and involve no more physical exertion than it takes to stumble the 50 yards between parked car and so-called lake.

When the first commercial fishery appeared near me I fished it once, out of curiosity only. I could almost feel Venables, Walker and the rest of them sighing in disgust as their erstwhile disciple walked down to the parody of a lake. It was square; its banks were flat; it had the occasional stunted willow and one bed of tired reed mace; the water had the scummy slick of used washing up water; the depth was uniform, and rats scuttled through the litter behind me. The place was an affront to everything I love about my sport. And the fish? Uniform, hungry carp with torn mouths: fish which were almost certainly reliant on anglers' baits to sustain them, so overstocked was the water. In ecological terms it was as balanced an environment as the average chicken farm.

Because I do not subscribe to the 'it's just my humble opinion' school of equivocation, where colours are so cravenly nailed to the mast, I am happy to condemn commercial fisheries without reservation. Not only are they a denial of most of the core values of angling, they cater for a market which demands instant gratification without effort. Maybe it's a Thatcherite legacy? Or perhaps it is all I should expect from a nation that consumes junk food with such enthusiasm? Junk sport then, for the terminally unimaginative? And this matters, not only on aesthetic grounds, not only on the ground that such waters will produce fishermen without skill or knowledge, but also on the ground that they are such an obvious target for the groups who oppose fishing. Ernest Hemingway used to shoot live pigeons in competition at Monte Carlo, a so-called sport that has long since been banned. Is the current enthusiasm for metaphorically shooting fish in a barrel really any different?

We seem now to have produced a generation of anglers who judge waters not by their beauty nor the quality of the fish, but by their accessibility, the bounteousness of their overstocking, the cleanliness of their toilets and the quality of bacon sandwich from their on-site catering van. Letters are written to complain about the fact that some waters involve a longer walk than is now acceptable, or to bicker about the fact that others have car parks without the nannying comfort of CCTV. The disability card is played – shamefully – to justify the cancerous growth of commercial waters. Not every water is accessible to all, but the disabled anglers I know relish their enthusiasm for fishing wild waters in wild places. My good friend, Steve Hardy, who has had multiple sclerosis for a number of years, seizes his opportunity to wade a fast-flowing river, supported by a wading stick, and he fishes hard and well. He may pay the price in the tiredness he feels the next day, but it is an affordable one for such an affirmation of life.

Many of the people I encountered on the lower floors were youngsters, me included. I started to fish at five, and fished without supervision from seven or eight. A couple of years later I would disappear to lakes miles from home, often without telling my parents where I was going other than the generic 'gone fishing'. My parents may have had their own foibles, but their acceptance of their son's long absences was quite normal. I was not in danger, even if I got wet and often cut myself on sharp branches and broken glass in the way that kids do. And once a middle-aged man tried to persuade me to let him run me home in his Morris Oxford, but accepted the suggestion that he should fuck off. How could I take seriously a threat from a man in a brown trilby and a shiny grey suit jacket? There are no more paedophiles now than there were then, but, thanks to the hysteria of the *Daily Mail* and the other red-tops, every mother believes that a pervert lurks on every corner and stalks the banks of every lake and stream. Moreover, these are places that, as every good parent will tell you, should also be avoided because of their dirtiness and their production of mosquitoes on an industrial scale. What do they worry about – malaria?

We live in a society which has become so averse to risk that the slings and arrows of daily existence are treated as threats to be avoided, and, if encountered, to justify litigation, righteous indignation, post-traumatic stress and a public apology from the relevant government minister. Which is why the average age of club and syndicate members in my area is nearer fifty than thirty, why I have to draft ludicrous disclaimers for my fishing club rule book, and why I fear that this sport will decline into a minority interest within the next twenty years. Unless, of course, fishing can be made sexy. Carp fishing can be – big fish, tough talk, expensive toys to buy – but youngsters soon grow out of it. Sea fishing? Sexy if you live in bone-fish country, but the prospect of casting a bait into a fishy desert off some joyless east-coast beach does little to allure. The commercial coarse fisheries? They reflect the market; they are safe, predictable and offer a guaranteed product. If McDonalds made lakes they would be like this. But great cooks don't learn their craft flipping burgers or dunking donuts, and great anglers are not created by the repetitive tedium of hauling out tame fish.

The rock and roll fishing, the new black, is (or at least could be) fly fishing, and here's why.

Thanks to the sport's popularity in the USA and the inevitable influence on our domestic sport, fly fishing is now being marketed and perceived as another extreme sport, as if it were an alternative to snowboarding, parascending or bungee jumping. Ignore the fact that an afternoon spent on a typical British trout river may be a pleasure, even a joy, but, unless you hook the unexpected 5lb brownie, is unlikely to overload your nervous system with adrenalin. British trout fishing doesn't tend to involve extremes, either of weather, fish or wildlife. I may see the odd roe deer, an osprey if I am lucky, but I have yet to be threatened by a grizzly or bullied by an elk on the Swale. But that inconvenient reality does not compromise the imagery, the iconography of fly fishing as portrayed by most of the fishing press and nearly all the mail-order tackle suppliers. The pictures in the advertisements show square-jawed hunks baring their pearl-white teeth into a Patagonian gale, or scowling aggressively as they set the hook into a permit, tarpon or fast-running barracuda. And this extreme universe is also populated by alluring twenty-something blondes, squeezed into tight-fitting waders and smiling demurely from under their Microfibre Bill Hats as they cast a dry fly on a Colorado spring creek. If any of these delightful creatures would like to experience the joys of a day on the Rye my phone number is available from the publisher, but I do not think the queue would be a long one. Such is the gulf between how fly fishing is practised and how it is portrayed.

The sexy pictures are complemented by even sexier copy. Who could possibly fail to be seduced by the appeal of a 'Polartec® Powerdry® Fleece, the Rivertek® ™ Heavy Weight zip top and grid pant'? (That's a hell of a specification for a pair of fishing trousers with a matching top.) Or how about a bag with 'ballistic nylon and 420 pack cloth exterior', not to mention the 'adjustable gunwale holes integrated into back-zipped pocket'? Bag or weapons system? Or a reel 'milled in T6061 prime grade aircraft aluminium'? (Why not the T6062 – just too much firepower?) Face it, you could start a small war with this stuff and feel confident that victory was yours, such would be the overwhelming superiority of your ordnance.

I am in my fifties, and I fall for some of this tempting prose too; I convince myself that I need a more technical wader or a rod with a modulus positioning system. Don't know what they are but they sound indispensable and will impress my friends. It is no different to my need to have a car with as many acronyms as possible in its specification, or to mention to a friend, *en passant*, how the performance of my Linn hi-fi is so demonstrably superior to the competition. And whilst some of what the technology offers is necessary, its only currency tends to be in extreme fishing in extremely expensive places to fish.

But what a contrast this is to how fly fishing used to be – it was how your Latin teacher spent his holidays in the Lake District. And instead of Explorer Pants and Soft Shell Jackets he would have settled for the wet dog comfort of pipe-smoked tweed and the weight of cavalry twill. He would have fished a split cane rod inherited from his father, and into his shoulders would cut the strap of a wicker creel.

And the first time I ever saw the sport practised was on the River Nidd in the early 1960s; I watched a fisherman fishing towards my bank, casting with a precision which was startling but with a purpose which was incomprehensible. No sooner had the fly landed on the water than it was recast slightly further upstream; it was busy, manic even, but it looked like an activity which had no discernible purpose, a means whose only end was itself.

But when I learnt how to do the same thing – felt what it was like to outwit a smartly placed trout, felt how it was to play a strong fish in a fast current, felt how the fly line ripped out over clenched fingers, saw it disappear into the swirling waters at the head of a pool, arrowing in stabs and jerks as the fish fought, saw what it was like when a 2lb trout crashes out of the water with the sun making rainbows in the spray – I understood. But until I saw all that, felt all that, I didn't get it. I do now, though, and the hope I have is that the imagery of the sport is enough to lure and to hook a new generation of anglers young enough, smart enough, committed enough and tough enough to keep the faith, to develop the sport, to fight for it and convert others to its practice.

And part of the fight would be to engage the public and to educate it into supporting an activity which conserves priceless habitat of both fauna and flora and enables an insight into species whose very existence is unknown to most of the public. I was first subject to a tirade of anti-angling abuse at York University in the early 1970s; it was as vitriolic as it was unexpected but seemed harmless, the actions of a student radical eccentric. But the insidious growth of the animal liberation lobbies has produced a strain of single-issue fanatics who surf on a great wave of self-righteousness as they fight to protect the interests of animals by such selfless acts as releasing thousands of rainbow trout into brown trout habitat, or freeing rapacious mink to wipe out vole, fish and kingfisher. Fanatics don't let the facts get in the way of opinion, and we are vulnerable. Of course there is the leaden irony of uninformed public opinion (it seems to me that the more uninformed the opinions are likely to be, the more they are sought and valued by the media), but where is the value in being told 'Well, yes, fishing is sort of cruel, I suppose, and I think it ought to be stopped because people shouldn't hurt animals' by a bleeding heart suffering from advanced anthropomorphism. That heart may beat in a body that patronises a stack'em-high, sell'em-cheap supermarket and ambushes cut-price ersatz meat produced by the type of agribusiness where animal welfare is suppressed by big profit margins and low overheads.

The same ignoramus will often ask his one-trick pony of a killer question, usually phrased: 'And how would you like to have a hook stuck in your mouth?' Faced with such withering cross-examination, my only response would be to ask my interlocutor how he would feel if he were blessed with a single-figure IQ, forced to live at the bottom of a cold dark river, terrorised by pike and pursued by piratical cormorants, limited to having sex only in the second week in October and having to look forward to a meal of cold caddis and wriggling shrimp – again. Faced with that lifestyle, I might just relish a change from the routine.

But, hey, now I am being anthropomorphic too – and not for the first time in these pages, I will confess. Consistency is such a leaden virtue, though – this book is about how it feels, remember, and feelings tend to run for the bus with self-contradiction on the destination board.

CHAPTER TWENTY-ONE

EXCHANGING THE IFS

Man partly is and wholly hopes to be

ROBERT BROWNING, 'A Death in the Desert'

O N ONE OF MY infrequent visits to London, whilst perfecting my hick from the sticks amble along Oxford Street, I almost collided with George Melly. His appearance would have caused traffic chaos in Thirsk Market Place, as it was as cosmopolitan as his surroundings. He wore a broad-brimmed hat, angled just so, an effervescent cravat and a suit in a shade of maroon which was on the startling side of distinctive. I experienced that irritating phenomenon of celebrity which makes us believe that TV exposure is a two-way thing, makes us think that they know us as well as we know them. I stopped myself booming 'Morning, George' but I did smirk a rather knowing smile. Not about his colourful past, nor his music, nor even the flamboyant cut of his sartorial jib, but about his relationship with trout, and one trout in particular. In his fishing autobiography he recounts the story of the capture of a trout which moved Good Time George to such transports of pleasure that he felt compelled to masturbate, either over or adjacent to the trout (I cannot recall which, but I bet the trout can), whose day was clearly going from bad to worse. I will allow that the reverse has happened to me, with fish spraying me with milt or eggs – but not, I suspect, triggered by an act of passion for the captor.

But the serious point is that, whilst I have yet to meet anybody who wanted to emulate the spontaneity and depth of George's enthusiasm, there is, if not an empathy, perhaps the remotest flicker of recognition of the joy which this sport can create. There are moments which can feel so perfect, so right, as to be unimprovable, transcendent of their context. It is a sort of Nirvana, and, whilst you cannot plan such moments you can learn how to recognise them, and, when you do, you wonder why life cannot feel so good the rest of the time. Happiness is a feeling of relaxation, a release of tension when you know you would rather be nowhere else than here, doing nothing else, than this, now. It is that rare phenomenon – a complete absence of desire. And, for a species driven – compelled – by desire, to experience its absence can feel like standing in the eye of a hurricane. We have all felt the phenomenon, if not often enough, and whilst it has a relevance outside the piscatorial, it does sound a particular resonance for every fisherman who has learnt truly to enjoy. In this sport so steeped in optimism and hope, do you prefer anticipation to hone your hunger, or realisation to sate it? The trick is to feel both – and the last time I felt that balance was on a late spring day on a small island below Rievaulx, whose eponymous abbey was visible a mile to the north over fields studded with hawthorns, each one champagned in the yellow-white blossom of spring. The main river takes the southern course around the island, and a narrow sidestream the northern. In places small enough to step over, the sidestream runs 70 yards east before rejoining the main river in a deeper pool, cradled by sycamore and alder. Spring arrives late here, and the leaves still have that pale green translucence, almost shining in their newness. The temperature is warm enough for me to have left my jumper in the car for the first time this season, and my sleeves are rolled up to catch that first exquisite burn from sunlight that has replaced the tentativeness of April with the assertion of May.

I hear the monotone rumble of a 747, high-flying north 5 miles above me, en route to the New World. Ryedale should be a place of peace, immune from real-world reminders elbowing my reverie. I shake my head and I smile at the memory of the July afternoon last season, when the Hercules transport had blundered its way down the valley, 300 feet up, pitching and yawing as it tracked the Rye's course. Was its pilot using this place – my private haven – to replicate some mortar-blasted wadi in Afghanistan, to practice his technique for ferrying supplies into some Taliban-enfiladed horror story? I remember how the Jaguar jets appeared later that day, just when I was feeling the first cool rush of the river as I waded in to the bottom pool, how they clawed the sky apart in a Doppler smear of noise, how they had cloaked the riverbank with their kerosene reek. And that day in the winter, half a mile downstream of the steep arch bridge, where I had found the mortar shells lying on the gravel bank. They were newly exposed by the December flood and were bleached and polished like old bones, footnotes from another conflict, when the estate had been used as a military training area during the last World War. The ordnance was still live, lethal, still hungry to remove a limb: collateral damage from a conflict which belonged to another century. *Et in arcadia ego.*

But now there are no threats, no man-made noises, now that the chainsaw from the forestry plantation has ceased. Birdsong is everywhere, punctuated by the metronomic call of chiffchaff and, just now, by the bisyllabic twitter of a pair of kingfishers arrowing downstream. I hear them just in time, and I see the sunlight enrich their blue to a diamond lustre. I can hear the quickfire rap of a woodpecker high up on the hill to my south and a sigh of wind in the higher trees above me. I hope to hear the curlews again soon; I had seen a pair wheeling and agitating over the last field, crying that call which makes loneliness feel companionable, company feel superfluous. River running free, you know how I feel; river audible, not just as white-noise background but as a whole symphony of splashes, rushes and hisses as the water fizzes and sparkles over rock and root. I can smell the water too, overlaid by the piquancy of wild garlic and the miasma of bluebell and raw earth, and my hands still have that sharp taint of trout. I am lying on my back and I am happy. I have fished for two hours, seen the dry fly attract a dozen fish, played a 1¼lb brown trout through two pools and taken three fish in three casts from the last sunny pool before I entered the tighter valley, where the dark pools begin. There are more pools to look forward to, but I know – and I am finding it surprisingly easy to accept – that this moment, when I am already savouring the immediate memory but honing my anticipation for the next, is truly as good as it ever can get.

But then I think of the last time I fished this stretch – when I turned the corner into the long pool with the current coursing under the willow over the fine gravel – where I could still see the rocking swirl of the trout which was picking off the olives one by one. I decide to walk up there in a minute, but not yet, not for a moment. Silence . . . Peace . . . My heart relaxes between beats, and the weight on my shoulders – the gravitational pull of regret – has been lifted. I am weightless again, and the future is as absent as the past because now . . . now just is. The prospect of the trout can remain just that – because at a moment like this, in a place such as this, I am happy to exchange all the ifs for the is. The moment has captured me and I it. *Carpe diem.*